INDIA: FIFTY YEARS AFTER INDEPENDENCE

T0307250

INDIA: FIFTY YEARS AFTER INDEPENDENCE

EDITED BY

KATHLEEN FIRTH AND FELICITY HAND

PEEPAL TREE

First published in Great Britain in 2001
by Peepal Tree Press Ltd
17 King's Avenue
Leeds LS6 1QS
England

ISBN 0 900715 40 6

Thanks are due in particular to the Universitat de Barcelona
who provided funding for this publication.

CONTENTS

III
Indians Abroad

IV
India On The Move

PREFACE

Just over two years ago we embarked on an adventure that was to provide us with an enormous amount of personal and academic satisfaction. Realising that 1997 was to be the golden jubilee of the independence of India and Pakistan, we both felt that such a historic occasion could not go by without Spain, and in particular, Catalunya, adding its own grain of sand to the celebrations that would take place in the subcontinent. As anybody who has organised an international conference will know, there were many headaches and moments of despair when we felt that the best thing to do would be to abandon the project altogether, but we soldiered on and we are delighted to say that the conference was a huge success. Inspired by the Barcelona conference, a group of participants decided to commemorate the historic event of the fiftieth anniversary of India's independence from Britain by publishing a volume of essays. Memories of the stimulating talks and friendly multicultural atmosphere still remain but our idea was also to reach out to the public at large, especially in Spain, where people's interest and curiosity about India is on the increase. More and more books by Indian authors are being translated into both Spanish and Catalan and the subcontinent is gradually becoming more familiar to the Spanish traveller, reader and consumer in general. The title of the volume, *India: Fifty Years After Independence*, should be understood as a tribute to the whole of the subcontinent, "India" being used loosely for brevity's sake and because of the tremendous diasporic experience of so many people of South Asian origin. Needless to say, we have not forgotten that Pakistan came into being at precisely the same time that India embraced independence.

The volume is organized around four thematic areas: Female Voices, the Storytellers, Indians Abroad and India On The Move. The volume opens up with three articles celebrating the emergence of long silenced women's voices in Indian literature. Murari Prasad traces the evolution of feminism, as it is understood in the subcontinent, from the early stages of independence up to the present. His essay includes references to women writing in autochthonous Indian languages as well as to already well-known authors such as Anita Desai and Shashi Deshpande, writing in

English. Mary Condé and Elizabeth Russell concentrate on anglophone women writers. Condé discusses the now troublesome relationship between India and English language and literature, while Russell delves into identity politics and the very notion of "home".

The second section, "The Storytellers", opens with an essay by the doyen of English studies in India, C.D. Narasimhaiah, whose contribution greatly enhances this volume. He provides a background for what was unfamiliar terrain to many people in Spain. Syd Harrex analyses the work of R.K. Narayan, one of the "Big Three", thus complementing Professor Narasimhaiah's homage to the other two founding fathers of Indian writing in English, Mulk Raj Anand and Raja Rao. Finally, Savita Goel looks at one of the most exciting and innovative voices of contemporary Indian and world fiction, Rohinton Mistry, whose novel, *A Fine Balance,* chronicles a grim episode of recent Indian history.

Our third section is devoted to those citizens of the subcontinent who, for historical, social or purely economic reasons, have settled in other parts of the world. Kathleen Firth looks at the twice-displaced Indian writer, M.G. Vassanji, whose work has flourished, like that of other diasporic Indians, in a Canadian context. Ranjana Ash focuses on the work of women of Indian descent currently working in Britain. Her essay is a survey of both the cultural richness and the restraints of tradition that define the creative writing of these women. Felicity Hand provides a brief history of the Asian community in Britain and through examples from the work of Gurinder Chadha and Hanif Kureishi suggests that Indianness has become an essential part of contemporary Britain.

The fourth section of the volume is dedicated to the strength and dynamism of Indian politics and the media. Somdatta Mandal pays tribute to Bengali writers in their contribution to the formation of a nationalist spirit in the colonial period. Daya Thussu provides a detailed survey of the evolution of the media in India since independence up to the late nineties and, last but not least, Sara Martín analyses Western images of India in contemporary cinema in the hope that Indian films will soon become better known abroad.

This volume is our modest contribution towards the furthering of multicultural exchange and understanding between India and our country as we approach the new millennium.

Kathleen Firth
Felicity Hand

Barcelona, September 1998

ACKNOWLEDGEMENTS

We wish to express our gratitude to the following people and institutions for their financial support in the preparation of this volume:

Ministerio de Educación y Ciencia
Programa Sectorial de Promoción General del Conocimiento

Generalitat de Catalunya
Comissionat per a Universitats i Recerca

Sr. Jaume Giné, Direcció General de Relacions Exteriors, Generalitat de Catalunya

Sr. Luis Valeriano González, Consulat General de l'India, Barcelona

His Excellency the Ambassador of India to Spain, G.D. Atuk.

Universitat Autònoma de Barcelona

Universitat de Barcelona

I

FEMALE VOICES

LITERARY MANIFESTATIONS OF FEMINISM IN INDIA (1947-1997)

MURARI PRASAD

D.S. College, Katihar

Indian feminism is not a direct offshoot of the feminist movement in the West. The usage of feminism as a blanket term to cover women's activism across cultures is not unproblematic, and as such it needs to be interrogated. As the meaning of womanhood is determined by cultural and temporal contexts, its social meaning is apt to be malleable. The perception of aggressive gender positioning flowing from popular notions of feminism and its attendant oppositional rhetoric is largely suspect in India. Few Indian feminists really contemplate overturning the status quo through their movement and abandoning the old order altogether. Of course they are advocating a better place for women in India by addressing specific gender perspectives and components, but their empowering strategies are much less drastic, much more Indian. It has been shaped by the native milieu and tradition and has had its own pace of evolution and growth. "I think Indian feminism is more practical than theoretical," says Anita Desai in a conversation with Lalita Pandit. It is " expedient rather than ideological" (Hogan & Pandit, 1995:168).

Gender consciousness has been evolving in India very differently from that in the West since the Bengal renaissance. In that sense, the feminist movement in India probably predates the American one. It was submerged in the freedom struggle for a long time. In that phase, women aspired to breathe liberation in the chains of tradition without closely questioning the patriarchal dispensation. During the years after India's independence in 1947, liberal nationalist feminism was neatly contained in the conservative programmes of the Congress government. The ameliorative agenda seeking women's uplift made tardy and piecemeal progress, offering fertile ground to women activists. No doubt the feminist movement of the Anglo-American provenance imparted momentum to the voice of sexual liberation in India and helped sensitize women activists to gender roles and patriarchal operations. As the movement stands today, "there are many similarities between the themes of the women's movement in India and feminism in the West" (Agnew, 1997:9). However, Indian feminists continue to resist the label and justify their stance as the one conditioned by their material circumstances and specific oppressions. Madhu Kishwar, editor of *Manushi*, a journal about woman and society, in an essay entitled "Why I do not consider myself a feminist," says that the term is associated with the colonial oppressors in the rhetoric of political leaders and in popular perception (Kishwar, 1991:38-40). Nevertheless, the cause of gender studies and gender justice in India would not have attained its current dimensions, as Andre Beteille notes, without the "presence of extensive networks" (Beteille, 1995:111).

The purpose of this paper is to focus on the articulations of Indian women writers and identify strains of gender perception proffered by some of the seminal and influential texts produced during the last fifty years. These works are not being studied as aesthetic achievements. Rather, they are being treated as cultural documents that manifest, define and extend alternative perspectives on life and society.

In post-independent India the restructuring of gender turned women activists back to the hearth and there was hardly any substantial change in their position. The optimism articulated by Sarojini Naidu, on her being elected president of the Indian National Congress Party in 1925, could not be sustained when the practice of the 1940s and 1950s in free India was in reality merely tokenistic. Here is Mrs. Naidu in her acceptance speech:

> In electing me chief among you, through a period fraught with grave issues and fateful decisions, you have reverted to an old tradition and restored to Indian women the classic epoch of our country's history (Sengupta 1966:177-178).

In contrast with Sarojini Naidu's enthusiastic appraisal is Dayani Priyamvada's observation on the state of women activists who took part in the peasant struggle in Telengana:

> ["As we worked among the peasants] we began to appreciate what a new society would be like with equality for men and women. After the police action and the elections to Parliament, these dreams were smashed. Crushed like an egg.... After the elections you know how we were, we were like the proverbial blanket which, when asked 'where are you now?' replied, 'I'm lying exactly where I was thrown'" (Priyamvada, Stree Shakti Sanghatana, 1989:73).

Not all women writers react to their subjugation and frustration in Priyamvada's vein, but even the diffident musings of traditional women writers bring out a sorry tale of female destiny. In the works of Shivani and Ashapurna Devi, we notice a gradual shift from tradition to modernity without any overt slant on shaking up the old order. Almost all the novels of Ashapurna Devi feature aspiring women-heroines, but she does not always endorse their aspirations. Her *Durer Jangla* (*Distant Windows*, 1972) brings out her comprehensive vision of feminism in the Indian context. Through Parboti and Romola, the novelist contrasts two versions of feminism. Parboti is a rebel within her tradition; Romola breaks with conventions and jettisons her roots. The latter is westernised and has no patience with traditional tools of emancipation. The former is also fiercely independent, but she is capable of sacrificing a lot for domestic harmony, whereas Romola is feminist enough to strike out on her own. Ashapurna Devi questions her choice: "Romola called disorder into her life. What was wrong in the cushy peaceful existence that she had been living. No one could understand that. At least, not her husband" (120). Ashapurna signals her approval of Parboti's homespun feminism. Yet she does not deny the existence of the Western brand of feminism exemplified by Romola, which is making waves in the Indian context.

While Shivani is cautiously modern without going against the grain of socially sanctioned attitudes towards gender, as we see in the story "Dadi" (Grandmother), her contemporary, Hamsa Wadkar, transgresses the restricted grid of feminine discourse with compelling candour. She aspires for a new kind of self-realization in her autobiographies published in the 1970s. She looks back at her life in the forties and fifties and voices her independent views on pregnancy. Eventually she ends up unaccommodated in mainstream cultural politics with her unfulfilled dreams.

Women writers including Rasheeda Jahan, Ismat Chugtai and Razia Sajjad Zaheer, inspired by socialist ideas, addressed the basic problems of life in the early decades of free India. Chugtai stands out among these writers in presenting varied aspects of middle-class women with their sexual urges, deprivations and emotional traumas. Her concern is articulated and finely etched in her novels like *Ziddi* (*The Stubborn*, 1941), *Tehri Lakir* (*A Curved Line*, 1943), *Masooma* (*The Sinless Woman*, 1961), *Saudai* (*The Crazy One*, 1964), *Dil Ki Duniya* (The *World of Heart*, 1966), and *Ek Quatra-e-Khun* (*A Drop of Blood*, 1975) as also in over a hundred short stories. Her exposure of social and sexual injustices is embedded in her detailed portrayal of the minutiae of the everyday life of men and women.

Rasheed Jahan's "Woh" ("That One") and Razia Sajjad Zaheer's "Neech" ("Lowborn") negotiate a new terrain of moral awakening to social responsibility whereby the marginalised women are imagined in new dimensions, but these tales do not seem to challenge the prevailing axis of power or patriarchal centrality. Susie Tharu and K. Lalita note: "In fact, there is a sense in which the education of these middle-class protagonists is also an education into strict paradigms that define gender in the reformist schemes of the progressive writer's movement" (Tharu & Lalita, 1993:83). Nevertheless, feminist articulations, if not with a conscious agenda, went on apace to loosen the levers of patriarchy. Sulekha Sanyal's *Navankur* (*The Seedling*, 1956) narrates the story of a girl growing up during the great famine and communally charged atmosphere of Bengal in the 1940s. It is a trail-blazing critique of the dominant gender paradigms. But such intermittent attempts could not bloom full scale as the progressive thrust of women's awareness seemed to run out of steam and it was not until the 1970s that emancipatory themes re-emerged in women's writing with clarity and direction. In the 1950s and 1960s, the ambivalence of liberal nationalist ideology towards women's lot was reflected in women's writings. Nonetheless, self-affirming women protagonists were portrayed by Indian writers in different languages. Krishna Sobti in Hindi, Ashapurna Devi in Bengali, Malti Chendur in Telugu, Dr. Indira Goswami in Assamese, Kamala Markandaya, Anita Desai, Nayantara Sahgal and Ruth Prawar Jhabwala in English and several others in regional Indian literatures present distinct feminist significations in their works. Sobti's *Daar se Bichudi* (1958) tells the story of Pasho, who has to yield to the sexual appeasement of several men, like an exchangeable commodity, for her survival. A perpetual victim of unequal social and sexual arrangements, she is rescued from her precarious situation and frequent dislocation by a newfound brother. In *Mitro Marjani* (1967), Sobti presents a much bolder and resistant character than Pasho. Mitro makes no bones about her sexual dissatisfaction with Sardari. She is wilful and defiant and ready to fly in the face of conventional constraints on women, in particular her jealous guarding by her mother-in-law. The assertion of female desire by Mitro exposes fissures in patriarchal authority and Sobti seems to be endorsing the rebellious mood of her women protagonists. Her latest novel, *Dilo-Daanish* (1993) resonates with the author's concern for women's situation in society, her sexuality and identity, her dignity and capacity to carve out a life for herself by defying orthodoxies in an intolerant milieu. Her protagonist, Chunna, asserts her individuality and emerges as the new, liberated woman from the suffocating ambience of early 20th century Delhi.

In her prolific fictional output, Ashapurna Devi continues to narrate the struggle of women without any ideological underpinning, unlike her contemporary Mahasweta Devi. Malati Chendur's novels, *Lavanya* (1968), *Meghala Meli Musugu (The Veil of Clouds*, 1969), *Brataka Neirchina Ana (The Survival-Specialised Seductress*, 1972) and *Jaya-Lakshami* (1976) explore the dreams and predicament of forward-looking women characters amidst contemporary social institutions. Portrayal of sexuality is forthright in the fiction of Dr. Indira Goswami, who has been by far the best-known feminist writer in Assamese for over three decades. Her protagonists affirm their right to self-fulfilment amidst hidebound tradition and brutalised masculine norms. The resurgent desire of her female characters and "the hazards of her existence", writes D.K. Barua, are the unfolding themes of Goswami's novels (Dhawan, 1995:56-82). Notable among her works are *The Current of Chenab, Ahiron, Rusted Sword, Blue Throated Braj, The Tusker's Worm-Eaten Howdah*, and a collection of short stories, *The Heart is the Name of a River*.

Among the Indian women writers in English of the post-independence period Anita Desai, Nayantara Sahgal, Rama Mehta, Shashi Deshpande, and quite a few others offer their perspectives on women. Kamala Markandaya's work is not overtly feminist, yet the condition of women shows through the overall texture of sociological realism. Rukmani in *Nectar in a Sieve* (1954) has had to take many things lying down because of sexual segregation and cultural prejudices against women. Her tolerance and placid, unruffled exterior conceals her suppressed aspiration for a liberated slot in her community. Society's preference for male children and the approval of motherhood depending on the sex of the offspring produced is an old indignity heaped on women by patriarchal norms. Mira of *Some Inner Fury* (1955), Helen of *The Coffer Dams* (1969) and Lalitha of *Two Virgins* (1973) typify the collision between tradition and modernity, and Markandaya renders the impinging of this conflict on women's consciousness. But it does not seem that patriarchy can be ruptured in her novels. Rather similarly, in Anita Desai's novels, the conflict between tradition and modernity takes the form of emotional maladjustment between sensitive female characters and their family setting. Her feminist awareness is concentrated on the emotional and psychic space which governs her protagonist's relationship with her immediate environment and social institutions like family and marriage. Maya in *Cry, the Peacock* (1963),

Monisha in *Voices in the City* (1965) and Bim in *Clear Light of Day* (1980) are passive rebels. By using the psychological strategy of withdrawal and alienation, Desai registers her critique of patriarchal cultural constructs and authority. In her novels of the eighties, *In Custody* (1984) and *Baumgartner's Bombay* (1988), she exposes patriarchal structures by moving in male protagonists to the centre and attacking outdated conventions thereby.

Unlike Anita Desai's women characters, Nayantara Sahgal's protagonists stand up for their views on morality, chastity and seek release from suffocation in marital bonds on their own terms. Sahgal's fictional world is also peopled by sensitive and sympathetic males who support free-ranging females, as we notice in *A Time to Be Happy* (1958), *This Time of Morning* (1965) *Storm in Chandigarh* (1969), *The Day in Shadow* (1972) and *Rich Like Us* (1985). The spectrum of women characters – with different backgrounds and different aspirations – is much broader in Ruth Prawar Jhabwala's fiction than in Desai's and Sahgal's. Though she has been criticised for one-sided depictions of Indian women – the depiction that "reinforces negative stereotyping of Indian women in the West (Hogan & Pandit, 1995: 169) – Jhabvala has immense gifts for conveying a variegated impression of the changing women's world in India over the years. In *Heat and Dust* (1975) she contrasts the silent women characters of 1923 with their self-willed and liberated parallels of 1975.

Rama Mehta's only novel, *Inside the Haveli* (1977), which won the prestigious Sahitya Akademi Award in 1979, endorses the central sanity and strength of compromise and adjustment in women's transition from tradition to modernity. Geeta's successful toning down of her modernising interventions in the Haveli is contrasted with Lakshmi's tragedy, underscoring the expedient line of feminism in India. In a perceptive analysis of the novel, Malashri Lal notes:

> Realistically, Mehta points out that upper-class educated women must provide the leadership to those born in less privileged conditions. For this they may need to sacrifice some of the modern principles of liberation that they could have grabbed for themselves (Lal, 1995:101).

Shashi Deshpande's women heroines are also quiet rebels. They find the conventional persona of wife stifling and struggle for individuation, but eventually they make peace with the family. In a recent statement of her intentions, Deshpande makes her feminist credo manifest.

It was with the articulation of all that had been in me through the year that I came to feminism, to a consciousness of myself as a feminist. I read a great deal after this – Simone de Beauvoir, Germaine Greer, Betty Friedman, Kate Millet, Virginia Woolf – whose *A Room of One's Own*, along with Beauvoir's *The Second Sex* have been the greatest influences on me. But it was not these books that made me a feminist; they were only confirmatory (Deshpande, 1996:103-110).

Deshpande resolves the claims and contests of marriage and domesticity, on the one hand, and the emancipatory aftermath of education and economic self-sufficiency of new women, on the other, by placing her protagonists along the middle path of enlightened conformity to tradition. Saru in *The Dark Holds No Terrors* (1980), Indu in *Roots and Shadows* (1983), and Jaya in *That Long Silence* (1988) attempt to break out of the persona fixed by patriarchal customs. Indu finds her husband Jayant domineering, without a semblance of sensitive reciprocities even in the sexual act. She turns to Naren and Akka for satisfying self-realisation and is finally reconciled to Jayant through a practical perspective on domestic peace. Saru in *The Dark Holds No Terrors* rebels against the demeaning round of heavily gendered prejudices practised even by her mother. She takes on an assertive role though her husband, Manu, will not let go of his restrictive hold. She returns to her parental home and reviews the domestic imperatives to find the parameters for her reunion with Manu. Feminist concerns pervade Deshpande's much-acclaimed novel *That Long Silence*. Jaya's silence and acquiescence to her husband's plans and preferences, and to patriarchal practices in general, form the main focus of this novel. Jaya's identity is reduced to becoming Mohan's wife and Rahul's and Rati's mother. She is renamed Suhasini in keeping with the tradition of giving new names to the bride after marriage in some Indian communities. But Jaya longs to traverse a different route to liberated womanhood. She prefers vibrant Maitreyi to blindfolded Gandhari among mythical parallels. In the end, to make life possible, she emerges into an integrated self and the novel ends on a note of hope:

> ...We don't change overnight. It's possible that we may not change even over long periods of time. But we can always hope. Without that, life would be impossible. And if there is anything I know now it is this: life has always to be made possible (193).

Feminist manifestations in regional Indian literatures are evident from

the 1970s onward with the growth of the women's movement into active
and dynamic political engagement. In the past decades, dreams of independence had remained unrealised in a large measure and there was much
disillusionment among disadvantaged sections of the population. The
1970s saw the mobilisation of marginalised groups in response to the failure of government to address India's diverse inequalities. Resistance to
institutional authority was revived with considerable polemical energy.
Women's activism got substantial boost from the emergence of several
forums across the country, such as the Forum against the oppression of
women in Bombay, Vimochan in Bangalore, Stree Shakti Sanghatana in
Hyderabad and Saheli in Delhi. With the publication of *Towards Equality:
Report of the Committee on the Status of Women in India* (1974) and declaration of the International Women's Year (1975), Indian feminism found
new campaigning energy. *Manushi*, a feminist journal started in 1979 by
a group of women in Delhi, proved an effective organ for women activists
to articulate and establish alternative perspectives. These women-centred
institutions won some battles for gender justice and provided new resources for feminist struggles in Indian society.

   Breathing the new social milieu, women writers came to size up current issues concerning their life and situation in India. Malini
Bhattacharya's street play *Meye Dile Sajiye* (*To Give a Daughter Away*) deals
with dowry murders and patriarchal oppression of women in India. It seeks
to rouse public opinion against the dehumanised, evil-ridden marriage system in the country:

> *Second chorus :*   If the bride and groom agree to marry
> It's simple enough! Why tarry?
> All this fuss for a dressing table?
> A wardrobe with a Godrej label? ....
> *Third Chorus :*   I say, everybody, did you know
> In wealthy homes it happens so –
> Pretty brides are burned to death
> when dowries prove inadequate?
> A stove bursts and goes up in flame;
> A death a day statistics claim.
> It's high time now you stopped those games
> Of seeking rich prospects with rich names.
> The times have changed and you must, too
> Or else these times won't forgive you.

Unlike Malini Bhattacharya, Nabaneeta Dev Sen does not invest her writings with radical feminist flavour; rather, she weaves in them delicately variegated feminist impressions. Her novel, *Shit Sahasit Hemantalok* (*Autumnal Abode of Brave Winter People*, 1990) is a melange of feminist reflections offered by an assemblage of housewives, working women and an established creative writer, an affluent woman of dishonourable past and other elderly women who recount their experiences and reflect on aging and loneliness.

The feminist concern takes on a striking dimension in the works of Mahasweta Devi. In Douloti, Mahasweta relentlessly exposes the exploitation of women bonded labourers. As Gayatri Chakravorty Spivak says, "... in Douloti it is the bonded prostitute's body that Mahasweta makes visible as graphic comment on the entire map of India" (Spivak, 1993: xxiv). Palamu and Gohumni show the resolute strength of these abused women to unite and retaliate against their bondage. Mahasweta drives home the point that the abolition of the bonded labour system by the Government of India is a far too inadequate measure to release all kinds of exploited labourers from the vicious grip of their masters. She is of the view that without a frontal assault on poverty, women cannot be freed from sexual oppression. Her social conscience on this issue comes out revealingly in another story, "Chinta," which tells the story of a wretched woman victimised by the entire web of iniquitous social and economic relationships. She is too poor to perform mandatory penance for the sexual act in which she has only a passive role. But it goes against the sanction of society and she has to sell her two infant daughters to re-enter the constricting orbit of her community. Mahasweta makes concrete the specific milieu of Chinta's miserable fate.

> She had no one. Her entire life pattern showed that she would have to keep on bearing the burden of the frail girl as well as the one to be born. This fact was amply borne out by the unflagging regularity with which she carried on her job. During the extremely chilly winter season she attended work clad in a soiled sari after having taken a bath at dawn; at the end of the month she had to remind the landlady for about ten days when she was given her salary of eight rupees. Understanding how helpless Chinta was, the landlady bargained stridently till the twelve rupees rate job was forcibly lowered to eight. Under all circumstances Chinta remained like an unprotected beast, tolerant and silent. Even when deductions were made from those eight rupees Chinta merely stated, "Ma has fined me" .... So I bribed my middle class conscience by giving

her some old clothes, or by handing over some tidbits to the little girl
...... In the process, my own little efforts to patch up my guilty conscience
became futile; patchwork was unacceptable in society (Trans. Sanjukta
Dasgupta, 1997:86-93).

Mahasweta pushes the boundaries of emancipatory feminist discourse
by portraying the actual material struggles of exploited women like Chinta
in the Indian context. Her exploiters range from men to her landlady to
her peers. Her situation and struggle foreground the inadequacy of the
Western feminist paradigms. Mahasweta's portrayal of tortured women
like Chinta, as Malini Bhattacharya notes, reveal a much larger pattern of
exploitation and offer "an exemplum of other issues" (Bhattacharya,
1997:1004).

Among other prominent feminist writers in India to probe and render
woman's situation and experience in society are Manjul Bhagat, Mrinal
Pande, Manu Bhandari and Maherunnisa Parwez in Hindi, Chhaya Datar
in Marathi, Veena Shanteshwar in Kannada, Vimala and Abburi Chaya
Debi in Telugu, Chudamani Raghavan in Tamil, Panna Naik in Gujarati,
Madhavikutty and Sugatha Kumari in Malyalam, Wajeda Tabassum in
Urdu as well as Krishna Bose, Mallika Sengupta, Jaya Mitra in Bengali
and Shobha De and Arundhati Roy in English.

To sum up, these articulations of feminist concern reveal many ideological cleavages on the issue of women's emancipation. Even as these
writers uncover the multiple determinations of women's situation, they
hint at new resolutions and alternative perspectives on gender, grounded
in the struggle for equality and justice. The outpouring of so many works
of fiction which express a feminist agenda is evidence that patriarchal
dominance is far from defeated, and women writers will doubtless still be
negotiating the challenging terrain of truncated liberation and unfulfilled
aspiration for some time to come. We notice, too, the ambivalent response
of society to these radical expressions of women's assertion. These literary texts bring new images to our social discourse, create sustenance for
women's aspirations and widen the avenues leading towards a just dispensation. Although the perspectives of these women writers are varied
and their affiliations diverse, they unfold new stirrings among the women
of free India.

REFERENCES

Agnew, Vijay, "The West in Indian Feminist Discourse and Practice," *Women's Studies International Forum, Vol. 20.* Jan-Feb 1997: 3-19.

Barua, D.K., " Manoni Raisom Goswami: The Insistent Pattern", *Indian Women Novelists*, ed. R.K. Dhawan. Set 3, Delhi: Prestige Books, 1995.

Beitelle, Andre, "Feminism in Academia: Changes in Theory and Practice", *Indian Journal of Gender Studies, 2:1,* 1995:111-113.

Bhattacharya, Malini, "Mahasweta Devi: Activist and Writer", *Economic and Political Weekly*, May 10 1997: 1003-4.

Devi, Ashapurna, *Distant Windows,* Calcutta : Mitra and Ghosh,1972.

Devi, Mahasweta, *Imaginary Maps*, Trans. Gayatri Chakravorty Spivak, Calcutta: Theme, 1993.

Devi, Mahasweta, "Chinta", *Indian Literature* (trans. Sanjukta Dasgupta), No. 178. March-April 1997: 86-93.

Deshpande, Shashi, *That Long Silence*, Delhi: Penguin India, 1988.

Deshpande, Shashi, *Indian Literature*, No. 175, Sep-Oct 1996: 103-110.

Hogan, Patrick Colm & Pandit, Lalita (ed.), "A Sense of Detail and a Sense of Order: Anita Desai Interviewed by Lalita Pandit", *Literary India*. New York: SUNY Press, 1995.

Kishwar, Madhu, "Why I do not call myself a feminist", *Manushi*. No. 63-64. 1991:38-40.

Lal, Malashri, *The Law of the Threshold*, Shimla: Indian Institute of Advanced Study, 1995.

Sengupta, Padmini, *Sarojini Naidu: A Biography*, Bombay: Asia Publishing House, 1996.

Stree Shakti Sanghatan, *We Were Making History*, Delhi: Kali for Women, 1989.

Tharu, Susie & Lalita, K. (ed.), *Women Writing in India,* Vol. 2. Delhi: Oxford University Press, 1993.

FINDING A NEW INDEPENDENCE:
INDIAN WOMEN WRITING IN ENGLISH.

MARY CONDÉ
Queen Mary & Westfield College, London

The relationship between India and English language and literature has long been a troublesome one. Writing in 1881, the distinguished man of letters Vishnu Krishna Chiplunkar epigrammatically declared that "Crushed by English poetry, our freedom has been destroyed" (Chandra, 18). Over a hundred years later, Gauri Viswanathan is in no doubt that what she calls the "nineteenth-century Anglicist curriculum of British India" was not only an expression of power, but served to confer power on the British rulers of India, and to protect them from a potentially rebellious subject population (Viswanathan, 167).

Ashis Nandy has pointed out the extent to which the cultural impact of imperialism was confined to India's urban centres, and to its semi-Westernized upper and middle classes. This is why, in his view, Britain as a relatively more homogeneous small island has been more culturally damaged by colonialism than India (Nandy, 31-32); it has also meant that the use of English in India has been particularly associated with an urban élite.

Renu Juneja writes vividly of the hegemony of English in her preface to her study *Caribbean Transactions: West Indian Culture in Literature*:

> Many, many years ago, when I began reading for Honors in English literature at the University of Delhi, fell in love with Keats, and recited John Donne to impress my friends, I could not have imagined that in my future would be a book like this one. I had fallen in love with language and literature, yet I could never imagine pursuing a degree in Hindi or Punjabi literature. Though I grew up in an *independent* India, I went to an English-medium private school, Queen Mary's School it was called, and forces of class and education dictated that all that was sophisticated and smart belonged to the medium of English. The phenomenon I am describing is very different from the sway of English as a world language which makes it a desirable acquisition no matter where you are (Juneja, viii).

Further, British colonial rule specifically empowered the academic critic, by providing what G.N. Devy describes as "a ready and vast market for critical texts", and endowing literary criticism with a significance it had never enjoyed before (Devy, 104). Despite India's low literacy rates (especially low for women) (Liddle and Joshi, 117), Rajeswari Sunder Rajan remarked in 1992 on the disproportionate emphasis on higher education, involving an expenditure of eighty-five per cent of the total outlay for education on two per cent of the population (Rajan, 20). Writing in the same year, Aijaz Ahmad finds the "parasitic intellectual dependence of the Indian university" at its most obvious in the teaching of English (Ahmad, 44). One consequence of this combination of circumstances is that Indian texts are given the metropolitan label of "third world texts", and are therefore implicitly required to perform specific tasks. As Ahmad says,

> The range of questions that may be asked of the texts which are currently in the process of being canonized within this categorical counter-canon must predominantly refer, then, in one way or another, to representations of colonialism, nationhood, post-coloniality, the typology of rulers, their powers, corruptions and so forth. There is no gainsaying the fact that these *are* among the great questions of the age. What is disconcerting, nevertheless, is that a whole range of texts which do not ask those particular questions in any foregrounded manner would then have to be excluded from or pushed to the margins of this emerging counter-canon (Ahmad, 124).

In addition, texts by women writers are required to interrogate systems of patriarchy. Yet they do this from a privileged, exclusive position. Even in *Savvy: Stories by Indian Women Writers* (Kohli, 1992), a collection specifically intended to break the stranglehold of English, whose fifteen stories represent fifteen different Indian languages (including English), five of the stories have been translated into English by the authors themselves. Indian women who can write with ease in English come from the affluent middle class and have had an élitist, westernised education, which determines their sensibility.

"Westernised" in this context is now as much American as British: Bharati Mukherjee, for example, in *The Holder of the World* (1993) draws heavily not only on the contemporary United States, but on Hawthorne's *The Scarlet Letter* and American colonial history. Padma Perera, author of *Birthday, Deathday* (1985), Indira Ganesan, author of *The Journey* (1991),

Shona Ramaya, author of *Beloved Mother, Queen of the Night* (1993), and Meena Arora Nayak, author of *In the Aftermath* (1992) all now live in the United States, and the first four of these writers teach at American universities. Anita Desai, whose latest novel is *Journey to Ithaca* (1995) and Gita Mehta, author of *A River Sutra* (1993), divide their time between Britain, the United States and India. Ameena Meer, author of *Bombay Talkie* (1994), divides her time between Britain, the United States and Mexico. Indrani Aikath-Gyaltsen, author of *Daughters of the House* (1991), Githa Hariharan, author of *The Thousand Faces of Night* (1993) and Sunetra Gupta, author of *Moonlight into Marzipan* (1995), all studied at American universities.

There is, in addition, a growing number of Indian expatriate writers in Canada. Anita Rau Badami, the author of *Tamarind Mem* (1996), lives in Vancouver. Her novel, however, makes very little use of a Canadian setting, since it is, like many Indian women's novels, essentially nostalgic, using the first narrator's emigration to Calgary merely as a framework, and moving back through the past to adopt her mother as second narrator. This mother, incidentally, who never leaves India, defends her decision to have her daughters taught in English rather than Hindi by asking her husband, "You want them to learn a different language everywhere we move? Bengali in this place, Assamese there, Gujarati somewhere else?" and declaring that "... without English, they will be like the servants' children" (Badami, 37).

Rukhsana Ahmad and Rahila Gupta, founder members of the Asian Women Writers' Collective which has produced two anthologies, *Right of Way* (1988) and *Flaming Spirit* (1994), defend their choice of English as a common language rather differently by explaining that

> English may have been the colöniser's language and a mark of privilege and class in our home countries, but here [London] it also enabled us to break out of our regional identities and make common cause with the other black communities and, for that matter, the different cultures that inhabited the term "Asian" (Ahmad and Gupta, xiii).

What is startling here is the assumption that it is beneficial for a writer to break out of a regional identity. It unconsciously reveals one of the many difficulties for contemporary Indian women's fiction in English, which might appear, indeed, to be boxed in on every side. It is the product of a very unrepresentative élite, is expected to have a particular agenda, and in straddling different cultures would seem to have sacrificed specific identities for a common cause so all-embracing as to be nebulous. In this connection it is interesting to observe the career of the novelist Shobha Dé, whose best-known work is probably *Starry Nights* (1991). Dé's novels, set in the film world of Bombay, do have a very specific identity, and (unlike many of the novels published in Britain and the States) use Indian words without self-consciousness and without a glossary. But it is only recently that there has been an attempt to promote Dé's novels outside India. It is, apparently, a matter of pride to her that her books are on the syllabus of London's School of Oriental and African Studies (Goldenberg, 9), but they have up to now been regarded as anthropological curiosities rather than as serious literature. The closest in subject-matter and setting to *Starry Nights* is Namita Gokhale's first novel *Paro: Dreams of Passion* (1984), published in London and very respectfully reviewed, but Gokhale's Bombay is bounded by English "dreams of passion", like the heroine's favourite novel, Daphne du Maurier's *Rebecca*, by which she charts her maturity (Gokhale, 111-112).

Some Indian women writers have made a determined effort to address the lives of Indian women who are not part of any élite. Examples of such efforts are Vishwapriya Iyengar's short story "Midnight Soldiers" (1987), Charanjit Kaur's short story "The Green Frock" (1993), and Kamala Das's collection *Padmavati the Harlot and Other Stories* (1992), which all focus on the brutalities of poverty, and Shashi Deshpande's novel *The Binding Vine* (1993), which investigates, in two parallel stories, the rapes endured by a middle-class Indian woman in the past and a working-class Indian woman in the present. The narrator's uneasiness about reading her mother-in-law's diaries is matched by her uneasiness at intruding into the lives of the working-class women she is trying to help, and we are made conscious that she is switching between two languages. Deshpande's own mother tongue is Marathi, but she only speaks it well, and English, which she learnt at about the age of four, is the language in which she invariably writes. It is perhaps significant that Mrinal Pande, who usually writes in Hindi, has used English for her autobiographical work *Daughter's Daughter* (1993), in which she is more concerned with her protagonist's earliest recollections, and with the emotional crises of a little girl, than with questions of poverty and oppression. Pande's choice of English here seems to be a luxury of which Deshpande is conscious, and on which she capitalises, in *The Binding Vine*.

Many Indian women writers have capitalised on their double sense of privilege and loss in using heroines who are in transit and dispossessed, because they belong to an élite. Nina Sibal, a diplomat who has lived and worked in New York and Cairo, and has now been posted to Paris, makes particularly brilliant use of her experiences as a visiting foreign representative in her story "Fur Boots", from her rich and varied collection *The Secret Life of Gujjar Mal* (1991) (see Condé, 1995). This story, in common with others from the collection, is highly unusual for an Indian woman writer in having a male narrator. Much of the fiction not only has a female narrator, or is narrated from a female point of view, but presents a female viewpoint as incomprehensible to or incompatible with that of the male. Examples of this are Ritu Bhatia's short story "The Smothering" (1993) and Pepita Seth's novel *The Spirit Land* (1994), which also deal with psychologically difficult transitions, from India to the United States and from England to India respectively. The English setting of the opening of *The Spirit Land* is comparatively rare in fiction in English by Indian women, although notable exceptions are Ravinder Randhawa's *A Wicked Old Woman* (1987), Atima Srivastava's *Transmission* (1992), and Meera Syal's *Anita and Me* (1996), which all take the Asian presence in Britain as a given. Manorama Mathai's *Mulligatawny Soup* (1993) does open in London, but is more characteristic in debating the merits of India for a woman born in England and of England for a woman born in India. A consistent feature of Indian women's fiction in English is that it anticipates an audience unfamiliar with India and – as does Dina Mehta's *And Some Take a Lover* (1992), for example – an audience unfamiliar with Indian history.

It is in this context that I should like to place Arundhati Roy's Booker Prize-winning novel *The God of Small Things*. First, Arundhati Roy is relatively unusual among prominent Indian women writers in English in that she is not an expatriate; expatriate experience, although it is a feature of her novel, is not central to it. But she does capitalise on her straddling of different cultures as an Indian writer writing in English, by making this a crucial element in the identities of the seven-year-old twins who are her main protagonists. Not only are we frequently reminded that they speak two languages, but they are "Half-Hindu Hybrids" (45), according to their Christian great-aunt, and Anglophiles, "Pointed in the wrong direction, trapped outside their own history" (52), according to their uncle.

The twins' world is plotted by a whole range of Western references, both literary and popular. Rahel expresses her love for her mother in a quotation from Kipling's *Jungle Book*: "*We be of one blood, ye and I*" (329). Estha is a devotee of Elvis Presley, and measures his moral worth by the yardstick of the film of *The Sound of Music* (106-107). On the brink of her fatal love affair, their mother is profoundly moved by Mick Jagger singing "Ruby Tuesday" (331-332). Chacko, their uncle, quotes verbatim from

The Great Gatsby, the story of another "Oxford man" (38). The daughter of
the Communist official, Pillai, recites Scott's "Lochinvar" as a party piece,
and both his six-year-old son Lenin and the seven-year-old twins quote
from *Julius Caesar* – although Lenin does not understand a word of what
he is saying.

The allusions to *Gatsby* and *Julius Caesar* reinforce the novel's central
theme of betrayal, whereas *The Sound of Music* and "Lochinvar" constitute in themselves betrayals, offering as they do utterly misleading stories
of beleaguered lovers who end happily together. After the twins have grown
up, they watch together, in a fragile and fleeting reunion, a dance performance at a temple which constitutes a reparation for betrayal: the dancers
are asking pardon of their gods for prostituting themselves to tourism (231)
by giving a performance which requires no human audience.

All the literary and popular allusions to which I have just referred are
readily intelligible to (say) an English, an American or a Canadian reader,
but such a (tourist) reader must also be familiarised with Kerala, the novel's
setting.

In an interview Roy said of her novel that:

> American publishers said I should explain more, that I was introducing
> people to "alien territory". I said, "Alien for whom?" I wouldn't open an
> Updike and want him to explain some American gizmo (Jaggi, 18).

But this is misleading on two counts. First of all, Roy is clearly familiar
with American gizmos, and does not need any such explanations. Sec-
ondly, she does, frequently, explain to her readers, for example that Baba is
father and Ammu *mother* (3), and that "In Malayalam, Mol is Little Girl
and Mon is Little Boy" (60).

Miss Mitten, the Australian missionary, is held up to derision because
she didn't even know what Malayalam was. [The twins] told her it was
the language spoken in Kerala. She said she had been under the impression that it was called Keralese. Estha, who had by then taken an active
dislike to Miss Mitten, told her that as far as he was concerned it was a
Highly Stupid Impression (60)

Miss Mitten is held up to derision, but at the same time we are pain-
lessly slipped the necessary information. We are indeed, and here probably rather painfully, slipped much information early on about who is
going to die, who is going to go mad, and so on; these two kinds of information are not unconnected.

Rukmini Bhaya Nair comments on the second kind of information: she argues that although Roy is right to reveal the outcome of the tragedy almost immediately, she kills off the wrong people. The dramatic irony of true tragedy requires that the hero, the one who carries the audience's hearts with him, dies. Annihilating Velutha (a god) or Sophie Mol (a stranger) is the equivalent of murdering the messenger or members of the chorus. What this novel really required was the death of Rahel (Nair, 6).

What Nair's argument illuminates is that Rahel does effectively die, psychologically and emotionally, as a consequence of the deaths of Velutha, murdered by the police, and Sophie Mol, accidentally drowned: two deaths for which she is made to feel responsible. Although the novel opens with Rahel's return, she is a true *revenant*, a ghost. Her brief incestuous encounter with her twin brother has little significance because he has already cut himself off from the world, so he is also effectively dead. The hero of the novel, the one who carries the audience's hearts, is the compound entity Rahel-Estha, an entity destroyed at the moment that the seven-year-old Estha is carried away on the Madras Mail leaving the seven-year-old Rahel screaming on the platform. Everything that happens after this, even Ammu's lonely death, whether we are told it retrospectively or in anticipation, is an anti-climax.

Like *Tamarind Mem*, *The God of Small Things* is essentially nostalgic; it looks back to an earlier time (precisely, December 1969) before the childhood world of the twins was shattered for ever, before "Edges, Borders, Boundaries, Brinks and Limits have appeared like a team of trolls on their separate horizons" (3). This means that the twins' knowledge of their world can be conveyed to the reader in a very straightforward, even naive manner, for example through their encounter with Miss Mitten. By the same token, what the twins do not know, for example about the boundaries between their family and an Untouchable, can be remarked on without compromising the relationship between writer and reader. The reader receives explanations quite unobtrusively, without, as it were, any loss of face, and maintaining the sense of collusion with Roy. The twins' mother is anxious about her children because

> To Ammu her twins seemed like a pair of small bewildered frogs engrossed in each other's company, lolloping arm in arm down a highway full of hurtling traffic. Entirely oblivious of what trucks can do to frogs (43).

Here we share Roy's, and Ammu's, superior knowledge of the relationship between trucks and frogs, and this superior knowledge is never vitiated by a lack of information about the nature of the trucks (in the case of these particular frogs, the caste system and the political situation).

This combination of an essentially nostalgic narrative with an unusual degree of deference to a foreign reader lays Roy open to charges of precisely that prostitution to tourism for which her dancers are asking pardon. These charges are the heavier, of course, because of the spectacular financial success of the novel, described by *Private Eye* as "*The God of Large Cheques* by Arundhati Royalties" (25). Indian reviewers in particular have found this financial success impossible to ignore. Michael Gorra opens his review:

> Here, with the cloud of a six-figure advance trailing behind her, comes Arundhati Roy (Gorra, 22).

Rukmini Bhaya Nair writes:

> I don't mean to be nasty, but few I imagine would disagree with me that had a whole chorus of Englishmen sung hosannas to Roy, but not paid up, it would have been difficult to secure for her the kind of reception she's got here, no matter what the merits of her book (Nair, 6).

Maria Couto remarks that

> the novel has been packaged and marketed to perfection with the kind of hype one has come to expect when Indian writing is taken over by the imperatives of international publishing (Couto, 73).

Geeta Doctor, alluding to Roy's theme of family secrets as well as to her commercial success, describes the novel as "the garage sale of the decade" (Doctor, 4).

John Updike, from his American perspective, entitles his review "Mother Tongues: Subduing the language of the colonizer", which suggests some kind of political triumph in Arundhati Roy's success (of precisely the kind Couto finds lacking), but his reference to "Occidental readers" ignorant of the continuing hegemony of the caste system (Updike 158) and his remark that "Treading Roy's maze, we learn a great deal about India" (Updike 156) suggest that the reader-as-tourist is alive and well. It is difficult to assess how far *The God of Small Things* may be essentially a tourist book in the sense that it is more satisfactory for a Western audience than an Indian one; all the critics I have quoted have found something to admire in the novel, although Rukmini Bhaya Nair is particularly exercised by the inaccuracy of Roy's Malayalam (6). Roy's winning of the 1997 Booker Prize was certainly not greeted with universal satisfaction in London (Glaister, 3).

It cannot be said that Arundhati Roy's novel has done anything to render the relationship between India and English language and literature a less troublesome one. In the process of capitalizing on her position as a member of a very unrepresentative élite, through the complexity of the fictional world she has created, she has, however, calmly discarded the specific tasks so deprecated by Aijaz Ahmad. She may have faked as well as constructed a new fictional identity, but she has managed, as Michael Gorra has observed, to produce that rarity in post-colonial fiction, a largely-conceived and ambitious book about private life (23).

The God of Small Things, a novel which itself turns on the iniquity of categories, appears to have escaped, through its various strategies, the tyranny of the "categorical counter-canon".

REFERENCES

Ahmad, Aijaz, *In Theory: Classes, Nations, Literatures,* London and New York: Verso, 1992.

Ahmad, Rukhsana and Rahila Gupta (eds.), *Flaming Spirit: Stories from the Asian Women Writers' Collective*, London: Women's Press, 1994.

Aikath-Gyaltsen, Indrani, *Daughters of the House,* New Delhi: Penguin Books India, 1991.

Asian Women Writers' Workshop (ed.), *Right of Way: Prose and Poetry by the Asian Women Writers' Workshop*, London: Women's Press 1988.

Badami, Anita Rau, *Tamarind Mem,* Harmondsworth: Penguin, 1996.

Bhatia, Ritu, "The Smothering", *In Other Words: New Writing by Indian Women*, Eds. Urvashi Butalia and Ritu Menon, London: Women's Press, 1993:66-79.

Butalia, Urvashi and Ritu Menon (eds.), *In Other Words: New Writing by Indian Women,* London: Women's Press, 1993.

Chandra, Sudhir, *The Oppressive Present: Literature and Social Consciousness in Colonial India,* Delhi, Bombay, Calcutta, Madras: O.U.P., 1992.

Condé, Mary, "Tourists and Pilgrims in Nina Sibal's Short Story Collection *The Secret Life of Gujjar Mal*", *Journal of the Short Story in English*, No. 24. Spring 1995:73-81.

Couto, Maria, "Accomplished debut: A novel that transcends limited perspectives" (review of *The God of Small Things*), *Frontline*, 16 May 1997:73-74.

Das, Kamala, *Padmavati the Harlot and Other Stories*, New Delhi: Sterling, 1992.

Dé, Shobha, *Starry Nights*, New Delhi: Penguin Books India, 1991.

Desai, Anita, *Journey to Ithaca*, London: Heinemann, 1995.

Deshpande, Shashi, *The Binding Vine*, London: Virago, 1988.

Devy, G.N., *After Amnesia: Tradition and Change in Indian Literary Criticism*, London: Sangam Books, 1992.

Dharmarajan, Geeta (ed.), *Separate Journeys: Short Stories by Indian Women Writers*, London: Mantra, 1993.

Doctor, Geeta, "Avenging Angel" (review of *The God of Small Things*), *Indian Review of Books*, 16 April - 15 May 1997: 4-5.

Ganesan, Indira, *The Journey*, London: Minerva, 1991.

Glaister, Dan, "The 1997 Booker Prize: Winning saga of love, death, lies and laws", *Guardian*, 15 October, 1997: 3.

Gokhale, Namita, *Paro: Dreams of Passion*, London: Chatto and Windus, 1984.

Goldenberg, Suzanne. "Pulp friction", *Guardian*. 26 July 1995:8-9.

Gorra, Michael, "Living in the Aftermath" (review of *The God of Small Things*), *London Review of Books*, 19 June 1997:22-23.

Gupta, Sunetra, *Moonlight into Marzipan*, London: Phoenix House, 1995.

Hariharan, Githa, *The Thousand Faces of Night*, New Delhi: Penguin Books India, 1993.

Iyengar, Vishwapriya, "Midnight Soldiers", *Truth Tales: Stories by Indian Women*, Eds. Kali for Women, London: Women's Press, 1987: 185-201.

Jaggi, Maya, "An unsuitable girl", *Guardian*, 24 May 1997: 12-18.

Juneja, Renu, *Caribbean Transactions: West Indian Culture in Literature*, London and Basingstoke: Macmillan, 1996.

Kali for Women (eds.), *Truth Tales: Stories by Indian Women*. London: Women's Press, 1987.

Kaur, Charanjit, "The Green Frock", *Separate Journeys: Short Stories by Indian Women Writers*, Ed. Geeta Dharmarajan. London: Mantra, 1993:167-175.

Kohli, Suresh (ed.), *Savvy: Stories by Indian Women Writers*, New Delhi: Arnold, 1992.

Liddle, Joanna and Rama Josh., *Daughters of Independence: Gender, Caste and Class in India*, New Brunswick, N.J.: Rutgers U.P., 1986.

Mathai, Manorama, *Mulligatawny Soup*, New Delhi: Penguin Books India, 1993.

Meer, Ameena, *Bombay Talkie,* London: Serpent's Tail, 1994.

Mehta, Dina, *And Some Take a Lover,* Calcutta: Rupa, 1992.

Mehta, Gita, *A River Sutra*, London: Heinemann, 1993.

Mukherjee, Bharati, *The Holder of the World,* London: Chatto and Windus, 1993).

Nair, Rukmini Bhaya, "Twins and lovers" (review of *The God of Small Things*), *Biblio,* May 1997:4-6.

Nandy, Ashis, *The Intimate Enemy: Loss and Recovery of Self Under Colonialism,* Delhi: O.U.P., 1983.

Nayak, Meena Arora, *In the Aftermath,* New Delhi: Penguin Books India, 1992.

Pande, Mrinal, *Daughter's Daughter,* London: Mantra, 1993.

Perera, Padma, *Birthday Deathday and Other Stories,* London: Women's Press, 1985.

Rajan, Rajeswari Sunder (ed.), *The Lie of the Land: English Literary Studies in India,* Delhi, Oxford, New York: O.U.P., 1992.

Ramaya, Shona, *Beloved Mother, Queen of the Night,* London: Martin Secker and Warburg, 1993.

Randhawa, Ravinder, *A Wicked Old Woman,* London: Women's Press, 1987.

Roy, Arundhati, *The God Of Small Things,* London: Flamingo, 1997.

Seth, Pepita, *The Spirit Land,* New Delhi: Penguin Books India, 1994.

Sibal, Nina, *The Secret Life of Gujjar Mal and Other Stories,* London: Women's Press, 1991.

Srivastava, Atima, *Transmission,* London: Serpent's Tail, 1992.

Syal, Meera, *Anita and Me,* London: Flamingo, 1996.

Unsigned piece, "Literary Review: *The God of Large Cheques* by Arundhati Royalties", *Private Eye,* 31 October 1997: 25.

Updike, John, "Mother Tongues: Subduing the language of the colonizer" (review of *The God of Small Things* and Ardashir Vakil's *Beach Boy*), *New Yorker,* 23 & 30 June 1997: 156-161.

Viswanathan, Gauri, *Masks of Conquest: Literary Study and British Rule in India,* New York: Columbia U.P., 1989.

LOCATION MATTERS: "INDIAN" WOMEN WRITING IDENTITIES AT THE CROSSROADS*.

ELIZABETH RUSSELL
Universitat Rovira i Virgili, Tarragona

In answer to some questions that miss the point
or
yes, but where are you from?

What I don't have
is a land
is a lover
is a language
to say, is mine

What I don't have
are ropes
of romance
of nationalism
of words to tie me down/in smug belonging
to stop me knowing
what more there is
Joyoti Grech, "In Answer to Some Questions"

It is no coincidence that much of contemporary feminist theory, relating to matters of location and identity, celebrates nomadism (Rosi Braidotti); cosmopolitanism (Julia Kristeva); migratory subjectivities (Carole Boyce Davies); and subjectivities constructed either in boundary-crossing, or at the frontier itself (Gloria Anzaldúa). This view of identity politics does away with the cult of origins and fixed definitions. It no doubt owes much to poststructuralist theories which destabilize identity, to the breaking up of totalitarian ideologies, and to the migrations of peoples in this century. It is a view which also, perhaps, connects to the political impact of peoples with multiple identities, religions and languages which make up the quilt of diasporas.

Yet, each one of us still engages in an attempt to fix identity. We take and collect photographs of ourselves, we write diaries and autobiographies, we go to the psychoanalyst or psychotherapist to find out who we really are and where we belong. We engage in a cult of the self, of our bodies and our minds. Identity and ideology overlap in many ways. According to Althusser, the subject is interpellated by ideologies that name and position her/him. We might think that we are consciously choosing certain subject positions, but it is the ideological state apparatuses that recognise us, hail us and define us both visibly, through repressive forces (such as the police and the army) or invisibly, through powerful institutions. Identity, in this sense, has little to do with choice and much to do with coercion and the discourses of power.

The nation-state furnishes its citizens with an identity card or passport which supposedly guarantees that citizen certain rights within the nation-state and protection abroad. How does one define a citizen, however? A British passport notes that only

> British citizens have right of abode in the United Kingdom. No right of abode in the United Kingdom derives from the status as British nationals of British Dependent Territories citizens, British Nationals (Overseas), British Overseas citizens, British protected persons and British subjects.

This confusing terminology makes it clear that power lies with those who define and makes victims of those who are defined. The written word – this brief text – hides many a tragic and painful story of the separation of families, friends, and lovers.

In Spain, we are all obliged to have an identity-card, which carries a photograph (face only, as is usual), our name, place and date of birth, address, our parents' names, our sex, our signature, our thumb and finger prints and our number. Location obviously matters. I am Spanish, according to my ID card. Born in India, living there for 8 years, I was then educated in schools in Scotland and South America, then came to Spain, married a German, and now have acquired Spanish nationality, and thereby am also a citizen of the European Community. How would I define myself? An Indian-born Scottish/British, Catalan/Spanish and European citizen? The question did not really bother me until I started doing research into location and identity politics. Through the various Erasmus and Tempus projects I have been involved in I meet more and more people with similar identities, whose "home" is both nowhere and everywhere. I – and they – have all been privileged in that we have not felt the need to go into exile, and not been forced to do so. Crossing boundaries has been a pure technicality, we have found homes and jobs wherever we decided to settle. Our children have not encountered any discrimination as second-generation immigrants. The theoretical debates on women and national identity that I have engaged with recently *are* rooted in painful experiences, which I have not experienced myself, because of my privileged position. The fact that I am appropriating the voices of these other women for this paper could be easily criticized. I prefer to lean on Gayatri Spivak's notion of "chromatism," where refusal to speak because I am privileged becomes an even more pernicious position than speaking out and risking counter-criticism (Gunew & Spivak, 1989: 416).

· Clearly, when talking about subjectivity, we must discuss boundaries between Self/Other, where the Other is subjected to Self but also becomes its support in the process of signification. The boundary between Self/Other can be transgressed, in a positive sense, as Hélène Cixous affirms in an interview with Susan Sellers, "The way to the other is less self and more other" (Sellers, 1986: 22). This space in-between, where meaning collapses, can be potentially creative in that new identities can be forged. But, the border or boundary can also be trespassed and then it may become an act of violence, in that the Other's space becomes violated.

The same applies for any discussion on national identity. "Defining" itself implies "to outline", "to limit", "to frame". "Identity" denotes belonging to the entity but is based on "sameness" rather than on "difference" (id: same) and thus becomes a politics of exclusion. In order to perceive common characteristics which link people, all differential traits are either ignored or rejected. National identity and definitions of race are cultural constructs which are fixed by nation-states in order to maintain borders and limits, and to grant or withhold citizenship. Nevertheless, the knowledge that they are not "natural" concepts means that the power of nation-states is neither inviolable nor omnipotent, but can be contested and challenged. The space in which these concepts signify can be transgressed and subverted.

Julia Kristeva writes in *Nations Without Nationalism* that the fragmentation of the self has reached such a point that we are at a loss when it comes to defining self. The consequence of this is that we either take refuge in a cult of national origins and religious roots, which may result in a hatred

of the Other, or we repress our own roots and indulge in a hatred of Self.
"Who are you and where do you come from?" may take us back to the
birth certificate, ID card and passport; all those legal documents that affirm our roots, but mean little when confronted with racism. National
and race prejudice is first based on the visible: Otherness is perceived
through difference of colour, and physiognomy. Eloquence and accent in
English may have the power to transcend class distinctions if the speaker
is white, but fails to have the same result if the speaker is perceived as Other.
As Rukhsana Ahmad and Rahila Gupta, two women from the Asian
Women Writers' Collective in London explain, fluency and eloquence in
English does not mean that you will be 'classed' accordingly, for the "British educational system is also spewing out a second generation of women
who [...] are working class because of racism and poverty" (Ahmad and
Gupta, 1994: xiv). Marginalisation resulting from the visible is one of the
themes articulated by Meena Alexander in *The Shock of Arrival*:

> After fifteen years in this country I now have an American passport. It
> has a color photo of me, clearly different from the black and white I had
> in my Indian passport, [...]. With this passport I can travel across bor-
> ders, enter this country without visa or green card. But what if I don't
> have the passport on me? And what difference will the passport make to
> my concern about walking on country roads where no other people of
> color are to be seen? My fear of coming across men in army camou-
> flage, toting rifles to kill deer, all the xenophobia of America sitting
> squarely on them, or bikers on Route 23 with big signs pasted to their
> machines: "500 Years after Columbus, Keep out Foreign Scum!" (Alex-
> ander, 1996: 65).

Meena Alexander's description of her passage of life in *The Shock of Arrival*, in which she writes of her cultural displacement, is also a reflection
on the importance of memory, and thus not only the importance of the
questions: "Where am I? Who am I?" but "hardest of all, When am I?"
Hard, because memory is "a burden of the past" with its cultural restrictions on women but, in the present, there emerges a voice, "a speech in-
scribed midway between terror – the tyranny of state, the wheel of worlds
into which a female body is cast – and the tenderness of elegy" (Alexander, 1996: 142). It is through the pain of remembering that Alexander's
artistic creativity is forged. An artist might strive towards the original
through the individual experience, but Alexander seeks uniqueness in the
postcolonial consciousness – a phrase that she uses – which is constructed

through alliances with other hyphenated identities: "the Indian Americans, Japanese Americans, Korean Americans, Chinese Americans, African Americans, Native Americans, Hispanic Americans, Jewish Americans, Arab Americans." (Alexander, 1996: 128). Debjani Chatterjee's "I was that woman" likewise invokes the communal memory of all women: Eve, Pandora, Sita, Mary Magdalen, cutting across cultures and across boundaries. Like Alexander, she speaks through, and with, a common voice:

> I speak in many tongues, my friend –
> Moulded by the black experience.
> Languages are my inheritance.
> I move in many cultures, friend –
> Of necessity I make them mine,
> Lightly treading in so many worlds.
> I dream the only dream, my friend –
> The glory that Martin Luther dreamt,
> Stretching from our past to our future.
>   (from "Voice and Vision", Chatterjee, 1989: 34).

This collective voice of "the black experience" links up women who have shared a common experience of colonialism and racism. Blackness, here used as a generic concept, has different applications in the USA and in the UK. For the former, blackness is usually applied to Afro-Americans and Afro-Caribbeans whose roots were linked to the experience of slavery and oppression. In the UK, blackness is less specific, ethnically speaking, in that it embraces all peoples of colour, but at a more explicitly political level the definition gives rise to tensions. The difficulties of establishing a common political agenda are visible at all levels: from the concept of universal sisterhood, right down to the definition of the self as individual.

When the Asian Women Writers' Collective was founded more than a decade ago, they decided not to define themselves as "black" but as "Asian", but their naming was challenged by women inside the collective who felt marginalised by the domination of South Asians and also some women who wanted to join the group but did not identify fully with the adjective "Asian". All collectives necessarily have to confront identity conflicts and power strategies, most of them originating in religious and cultural issues. Nevertheless, these tensions can be translated into creative art, as Meena Alexander stresses, when she refers to art "plung[ing] headfirst into the destructive element" and becoming an essential part of "collective nonviolent resistance" (Alexander, 1996: 163). For Alexander, the process of creativity involves a process of "unselving", tinged with a "subtle violence". Although the work emanates from the artist's own individualistic subjectivity, it "must enter the public space, rupture it, [and] rework community" (Alexander, 1996: 128). In similar terms, the artistic production of the Asian Women Writers' Collective went through the following stages: at the beginning, when the group was first formed, individual writers would read their creative writing aloud to the other members. A subtle hierarchy took shape which evaluated work according to quality or to literariness. This quickly gave way to a new group consciousness which focused more on support rather than on criticism. The inspiration and motivation to write, the construction of characters, and the process of editing and publication are now done collectively. It is not only the Asian Women Writers' Collective that has been active in this field, each year new anthologies of short stories, poetry and critical essays are published by large and small publishing companies. Introductions to these anthologies are written from the perspective of "we" rather than "I", focusing less on individual desires and lifestyles and more on "our varied and universal human experiences" (Choong, Cole Wilson, Parker and Pearse, 1991: v).

"Unselving" or deconstructing self in order to reconstruct self is the theme of the poem by Joyoti Grech which this paper begins with. Grech comes from a cross-cultural background, she was brought up to be conscious of the "richness of a double heritage" which taught her the "nonsense of 'nationality' and cultural exclusiveness" (Choong, Cole Wilson, Parker and Pearse, 1991: 132). In her poem, "In Answer to Some Questions", she constructs identity through a negation of attributes which tie down and limit, such as land, lover, language, romance and nationalism: all of them are "someone else's borderlines" which prevent knowledge of elsewhere, and prevent her from taking up a position of transnationality.

> What I don't have
> is pencil lines
> drawn around my/self
> by pale people
> who know nothing/of my terrain
>
> What I don't have
> are someone else's borderlines
>
> I rub them out with my desire
>   with action

and a need to know

I am never satisfied

I flood their borders
with the sea of my sisters' names
and my brothers
whose lives keep their blood
red like mine.

Grech's poem constructs a positive identity through the negative, through allowing the silence and the gaps to speak. Amryl Johnson, the Trinidad-born British poet in "They Came in From the Margins", plays with the connotations of the blank page, uninscribed identity and authority:

They came in from the margins
forcing an awareness centre stage
shaped their own patterns
burning a peripheral
decisive trail
Forms of resistance
demanded that I take stock
rephrase the intent
which separated the crawling will from the
scrawling force

came fast and determined
          (I cannot believe the vision
          which comes to me now!)

If the above lines were to be read in terms of national identity in Britain, and what it means to be "British", the poem might suggest that "Britishness" has been constructed according to the claims of so-called minority or marginal groups. Whether in the context of outside immigration from the Commonwealth, such as people living in the Falklands/ Malvinas, Hong Kong or Gibraltar, or in terms of secession within the British Isles itself, as in the case of Wales and Scotland, the notion of "Britishness" seems to have become an important issue through the challenging of those relegated to the margins (Jackson & Penrose, 1993: 9). If identities at the margins are not tension-free, as the introduction to *Flaming Spirit* (1994), the short-story anthology of the Asian Women Writers'

Collective in London, affirms, the question of which language to use to describe a postcolonial experience is even more problematic. The members of the group first began to write in their mother tongues: English, Urdu, Hindi, Punjabi, Gujarati and Bengali until English took over because "it enabled us to break out of our regional identities and make common cause with the other black communities and, for that matter, the different cultures that inhabited the term 'Asian'." (Ahmad & Gupta, 1994: xiii).

Blackness as a generic term has already been referred to above, but one of the most interesting aspects of Black and Asian diasporic women's writing is the concept of Blackness as home. In Western tradition, from John Ruskin to Freud, woman's body has been linked to attributes of the home, such as nurture, a place of refuge, the family and the familiar, the "heimlich" and the "unheimlich" or the uncanny. Nationalist politics exploits the ideological power of such terms as Motherland and Mother tongue. Nationalist exploitations of women's reproductive powers have either idolized the mother who can perpetuate the purity of the race, or execrated the mother whose sexuality and offspring defile the race. Women themselves are not innocent victims in this strategy, writes Kristeva, for "the biological fate that causes us to be the *site* of the species chains us to *space*: home, native soil, motherland [...]" can easily be manipulated. Over and above this, women who worship the *national language* and who are "sexually, professionally, and politically humiliated and frustrated" can fall into the trap of becoming "accomplices of religious fundamentalisms and mystical nationalisms" (Kristeva, 1993: 34). In the case of Indian women writing about their bodies as home, Rama Mehta's novel *Inside the Haveli* (1977) must be mentioned and also Meena Alexander's comment on her poem "Ashtamudi Lake" where she envisages the difficulties in moving between two worlds, a vision which ends with a "house filled with flames" and the risk of choking to death (Alexander, 1996:143). Who decides where "home" is?

British Immigration laws ironically dictated by the "Courtesy of the Home Office" become the laws of a nightmarish "Big Brother" which separates families and prevents homes from forming. Debjani Chatterjee's "Primary Purpose" narrates the humiliation of Asian marriages being nullified at the immigration desk, where the "politely paternal" officer, "Double checking the ink stains of marriage sheets", knows that "At least you will not reproduce / More Asian females to breathe this air of freedom, and fair play". Home is not always a place of comfort, but can also become a place of alienation and displacement, "homophobia", is – for Gloria Anzaldúa – a fear of going home.

For women torn between two cultures and two homelands, the cross-roads offers a liminal space where they can look in two directions at once, belonging to neither or to both, as it suits them. It is this position that Leena Dhingra's heroine in the novel *Amritvela* recognizes as a site of potential trans-gression:

> The non-stop flight to New Delhi is halfway. But only my watch in-forms me of that. Through the window we appear quite immobile, suspended over a vast expanse of curdling clouds. If, as I have often said, I feel myself suspended between two cultures, then this is where I be-long, the halfway mark. (Dhingra, 1988:1)

It is women, more than men, writes Kristeva, "who have the luck and responsibility of being boundary-subjects: body and thought, biology and language, personal identity and dissemination during childhood, origin and judgement, nation and world" (Kristeva, 1993: 35), although she warns them of certain traps which could condemn them to either nation-alist politics or world-oriented militancy. Amryl Johnson claims that space between home and elsewhere for her own:

> I could go back
> I could go home
> I could return to my village
>
> I pause at the crossroads
> to wait for the moment
>
> Could have gone back
> Could have gone home
> Could have returned to my village
>
> But the moment never came

REFERENCES

Ahmad, Rukhsana and Gupta, Rahila, *Flaming Spirit*, London: Virago Press, 1994.

Alexander, Meena, *The Shock of Arrival. Reflections on Postcolonial Experience*, U.S.A. South End Press Collective, 1996.

Choong, Da, and Olivette Cole Wilson, Sylvia Parker and Gabriela Pearse (1991), *Don't Ask Me Why: An Anthology of Short Stories by Black Women*, London: Black Womantalk, 1991.

Dhingra, Leena, *Amritvela*, London: The Women's Press, 1988.

Gunew, Sneja and Spivak, Gayatri Chakravorty, "Questions of Multiculturalism" in: Mary Lynn Broe & Angela Ingram (eds.), *Women's Writing in Exile*, Chapel Hill & London: The University of North Carolina Press, 1989.

Jackson, Peter and Penrose, Jan, *Constructions of Race, Place and Nation*, London: University College London Press, 1993.

Kristeva, Julia, *Powers of Horror: An Essay on Abjection*, New York: Columbia University Press, 1982.

Kristeva, Julia, *Nations Without Nationalism*, New York: Columbia University Press, 1993.

Rutherford, Anna et al., *Into the Nineties. Post-Colonial Women's Writing*, London: Kunapipi, 1994.

* I would like to acknowledge my thanks to the Spanish Ministry of Education which has financed an interuniversity research project on women's cross-cultural writing in English. This paper is part of the project.

II

THE STORYTELLERS

WANTED: THE CONCEPT OF A NATIONAL LITERATURE
FOR INDIA

C.D. NARASIMHAIAH
Dhvanyaloka, Mysore

I first began to be exercised on this business of a national literature in 1950 when I was at Princeton soon after my two years in England. How did the United States come to produce a national literature in the language of its colonial masters? I pondered. Will India have to wait as long after its independence? But, unlike the States, which had had to start from scratch – literally from scrap books of the Colonial period – India had a rich past with its foundations laid by the literature of Vedas and Upanishads, followed by the Epics and the masterpieces of the Classical Age of India, which glory gradually dried up before the end of the first millennium after Christ. It is futile to blame political invasions, for the country had withstood them all well before the Christian era and done great things in art, literature, science and philosophy in the face of invasions.

A little island without history, with a borrowed religion from the East (drained of its spiritual content), a borrowed culture and political system from Greece could nevertheless speak of "The Great Tradition" in poetry and fiction, with a mere 500 years to look back on. And India had everything which England and the States did not have, and yet we keep parroting the names of Valmiki, Vyasa, Kaldasa, Bhasa, Bhavabhuti from our distant antiquity and have not gone beyond this. Or, because of our complex linguistic situation, coupled with the deplorable absence of a critical climate, we are not aware that we have today done things which might well be worthy of our great past. Can we identify from our various languages titles which help to formulate a concept of a national literature? Are they worthy of serious attempts at translation into each other's languages (as indeed some of them have been translated into various languages) and into English? Is it just a question of finding the right translators – who must be very few for any language? I have read somewhere that Dostoevsky in translation appears in a more favourable light than in Russian. Does Shivashankara Pillai's *Chemmeen* in translation suppress the shortcomings of the original? Does the English *Gitanjali* drain all the poetry from the original? Or Karanth's *Whispering Earth*? But why don't the Upanishads, the *Ramayana,* the *Mahabharata*, or Kalidasa's *Sakuntala* suffer in modern translation? And so we need to break through the barriers of Time and Place, go back to the past of India and know what is done in our other languages in this country.

Within a politically torn Europe, T.S. Eliot felt impelled to insist that no writer aspiring to greatness in any one of the European languages could afford to be ignorant of what was happening in its other languages. This must come as a severe warning to our serious writers, many of whom are better acquainted with Camus, Neruda, Márquez and Nabokov than with their next-door neighbours. Taken together, do representative titles by authors in Indian languages help to gain insights into diverse aspects of Indian reality? I am thinking of 19th century American authors such as Hawthorne, exploring the implications of conventional morality in the Puritan society of his day in *The Scarlet Letter,* or Emerson and Thoreau calling attention to a centre of wholeness from the extreme materialism which threatened to betray the ideals of the Pilgrim Fathers and the American Revolution; or Whitman affirming and reaffirming the democratic spirit of his country; or Melville diving into the dark depths of the Pacific to test the undying spirit of man, which was interestingly followed up by Faulkner and Hemingway, who asserted that man could not only not be defeated but would prevail ultimately. Consider this against British provinciality. As someone vividly remarked: "The American literary schooner was scudding before the wind, with everything taut and ship-shape, while the British literary house-boat drifted lazily downstream with awnings and easy chairs and hammocks and flower-boxes filling its decks".

Does Indian Literature reveal such an identity? Within American Literature, Jewish writing has refused to get lost in the melting pot and has retained its identity. Parallels can be cited from Buddhist and Jain literatures and to an extent the Veerashaiva Literature, for all three are primarily characterized by an overriding Indianness – if only because they are derived from Hinduism and were simply rebelling against its accretions. But the spirit of rebellion is built into Hinduism itself, as for instance when the Charvakas were invited to preach godlessness from the precincts of our temples. (We could afford that luxury!)

Even a hasty reading I did of four books in preparation for a seminar: Bhattacharya's *Mrityunjaya*, Karanth's *Visions of Mookajji*, both winning

Jnanapith Awards, Aurobindo's *Savitri* and *Amma Vandaal* or *The Sins of Appu's Mother* (all of which can be read in English) show a remarkable Indianness in the manner in which the great Indian tradition is kept alive in each work. While reading Battacharya's *Mrityunjaya* in English translation I noticed continuous references woven into the texture of the work as metaphor, symbol, myth, allusion, analogy from the *Ramayana*, *Mahabharata*, *Bhagavata*, Buddha, Ramanuja, Chaitanya, Sankaradev, the Bhakti poets and the folk tales with considerable approval, whereas in Karanth's work the epics and their outlook on life come in largely for disapproval, providing what the novelist in his vision considers as healthy correctives to age-old practices. As for *The Sins of Appu's Mother*, from Tamil, it is not a moral exploration but an artistic attempt (I say 'artistic' because, after all, a great work of art is some kind of disguised sermon, fable, philosophy, persuasion) to bring light to the sinner. The light may come either in terms of traditional wisdom or by importing what is borrowed from other sources in the characteristic Indian way. As the Rigveda exhorted from earliest times: "Let great thoughts come from all directions". But today the borrowing has often degenerated into imitation or derivation, seldom assimilation on *our* terms. I shall not labour to present the argument of Aurobindo's *Savitri*, which is avowedly Indian in conception as well as in execution, though the poet has absorbed the great epics of the world into his creative self.

A reading of these books reminded me of the creative and critical endeavours of T.S. Eliot and F.R. Leavis. Eliot goes back to the minor dramatists of the Elizabethan Age, to Donne and the other Metaphysical poets, even to the Silver poets (some called them 'tinsel') of the Augustan Age in his effort to counteract the harm done to English Poetry by Milton, the dreamy Romantics and the ruminating Victorians. He writes about them in his criticism as if to justify his creative use of some and rejection of others. Leavis writes whole books tracing "the line of wit" in English poetry and "the great tradition" in fiction. This is the way a tradition is kept alive in a culture and prevented from degenerating into the dead wood which convention is. Imbibing the influence of Dante, Eliot takes note of some of the subtlest things. He says, for example, that Dante *thought* in *terza rhyma* and suggests that if you miss that fact you miss the fact that he had "a coherent view of the universe" and that "he thought to a purpose" in poetry.

This keeping alive a tradition is precisely what these Indian writers have done, including Karanth, who sometimes questions the values, at other times the modes of enacting them in the works. Moreover, to take an extreme case in fiction, I have noticed the process at work even in the ironic efforts of R.K. Narayan, who writes in English but with the Indian world-view at the centre, as becomes evident in novel after novel. Or he writes a successful short story like the one entitled "A Horse and Two Goats" with nothing resembling a plot but as an encounter between two individuals, an English-speaking white man and an Indian peasant, both representatives of the cultures to which they belong.

The most original of artists have invariably probed, discovered and re-discovered the old and revalidated it – old stone to a new building, old wood to a new fire... . Bawa, the painter who depicts Krishna enchanting a tiger with his flute, is neither repeating nor imitating but reaffirming the Krishna legend and taking it beyond where Krishna himself left it. R.K. Narayan could write a modern novel with *A Tiger for Malgudi*, enacting a very old fable and making it credible even to his Western readers. Likewise, Raja Rao uses the character of Savitri, now a very modern young woman (because the *yugadharma* [angst] demands it and anything else would falsify the character), not only to affirm old values but to go beyond the Savitri of the legend. Of her own volition, Rao's Savitri submits, somewhat grudgingly perhaps, to an old custom because she sees over-whelming justification for it, namely, the stability of society rather than the assertion of her individual ego – something which will be endorsed by modern genetic biology, according to which the accent is on the gene, not the individual.

But have our writers carried their art forms further as practitioners in the way James Joyce did through his "stream of consciousness" technique, D.H. Lawrence through his "blood consciousness", and T.S. Eliot, through his omnivorous appetite for knowledge, returning not only to the roots of his own culture but also borrowing what is valid in the primitive cultures of the world? And if they have, do we know of it? Eliot was convinced that the need for spiritual improvement in modern man was so pronounced that no one culture could answer to his complex present and he had to partake of mankind's heirloom. This explains why the distinguished Canadian writer Margaret Laurence virtually turns her face away from the British example, which she says has nothing to give her while Africa can meet her needs richly. It explains what Patrick White has done: received reinforcement for his own Christian upbringing from Gandhi's felt utterances on the nature of suffering, not as in Christianity to make a martyr of one, which runs the risk of hardening one's own ego, like the Archbishop's in *Murder in the Cathedral*, but in chastening the individual in the characteristic Indian way, because the individual must continue to live for *lokakalyana,* the good of the world, as seen in Laura Trevelyan's decision to become a schoolmistress and in her adopting the orphaned child of her convict servant, thereby calling for a return to Christian charity and to Upanishadic *Daya.* We may have much to learn from these examples.

How does criticism proceed to handle the literature before us? We have lost touch with our own critical principles, criteria, tools of analysis and critical terms and have been living on borrowings from the West which haven't proved their soundness; they are even known to distort our ends and means.

An important facet to which no one seems to have paid any attention is to remember that the Western mode is empirical – Aristotle being the original sinner! Unlike his master, Plato, who tried to formulate his poetics dialectically from first principles, Aristotle based his theories on the basis of his observation of prevalent practices on the Greek stage. Yet the entire Indian tradition of a thousand years, which, on the contrary, originated in an essentially Indian view of life and was strengthened by a succession of some of the finest minds, has suffered neglect, humiliation and even total rejection at our hands – and this, let me assert, without adequate examination. Here there are works in Indian Literature shaped by the Indian ethos even when some of them wished to run counter to it. Is it fair to judge them by non-Indian standards which are at times unIndian?

Allow me to offer a couple of examples from poetry and fiction. I have chosen works to which we all have access and which quite a few of us are likely to have read, or will certainly know of. First, Aurobindo's *Savitri* in poetry. In this work the poet turns to the Savitri story of the *Mahabharata,* which had figured earlier in the Vedas as a *mantra,* an incantation and a prayer to the sustaining Principle of the universe. Aurobindo takes this symbolic story of the conquest of darkness and death by light, of ignorance by knowledge – a concept profoundly central to Indian thought in its diverse manifestations in religion and philosophy. It is a magnificent conception and a colossal undertaking for a modern poet.

The poet seeks out this "area of darkness", which suggests very different things to him from what it does to men like Naipaul, for it is, if anything, akin to Eliot's notion of the "darkness of God". Small wonder, then, that the poet courts it as a lover does his beloved:

> I made an assignation with the night
> her dark and dangerous heart to woo.

These are lines of arresting audacity, because apparently he is cast in the heroic mould – he, a kshatriya, tapping the unconscious of his race in which a Viswamitra was striving for *brahmajñana* and the status of a *brahmarshi*. A whole intellectual tradition backs this endeavour. I cite two titles: one, a book of lexicography, a compendium of indestructibles, *Amarakosa*, the other, a book of grammar, *Sabdamanidarpana*. The lexicography opens with a *mangalasloka*, a prayer to Him who is an ocean of *Jñana* and *Daya*, Knowledge or Illumination and Compassion, and giver of *sriyaca* and *amritayaca*, wealth and happiness in this life and the life to come. Similarly, *Sabdamanidarpana* , the grammar book, opens with a prayer to Vagdevi, the presiding deity of language, and enunciates the object of the work as follows:

> The science of grammar brings the benefit of words, *padasiddhi*; *padasiddhi* brings *artha vicara*, inquiry into meaning which, in its turn brings *tatvajñana*, philosophical knowledge which results in the much desired *Moksha,* self-realization, the ultimate goal of earthly endeavour.

I mention this to stress how everything is geared to the recognition of the spiritual behind the material in Indian life. Even dictionaries and grammar books have for their goal this highest knowledge, a knowledge which to the poet of *Paradise Lost* is a "forbidden fruit", the cause of "all our woes" starting with "the loss of Eden". This is what Western man calls the vision of Evil. And evil is dispelled in that epic by a wave of the magic wand, in a tradition which, paradoxically, swears by rationality and empiricism, that is, by the coming of "one greater man who restored and regained the blissful seat" – a very simplistic solution, which is all right in a theologian but not in a poet whose first obligation should have been the *enactment* of the process of restoration in terms of art. Not surprisingly, Aurobindo observed that "justifying the ways of God to Man" is not the province of poetry!

As further comparison, let us consider the uses of the negative in the opening lines of both *Paradise Lost* and *Savitri*. Of man's first "disobedience" and the fruit of that "forbidden" tree, whose "mortal" taste brought "death" into the world and all our "woes" with "loss of Eden", etc. is a theologian's summing up in terms of "Don'ts", not a poet's perception in terms of images. Compare Milton in the same Christian tradition with one who was by profession a priest, Gerard Manley Hopkins, who had, moreover, set a low premium on poetry in comparison with sainthood and yet who eked out "the blissful seat" the hard way in poem after poem.

A stanza from Hopkins's "Wreck of the Deutschland" should help to make my point:

> They fought with God's cold –
> And they could not and fell to the deck
> (Crushed them) or water (and drowned them) or rolled
> with the sea-romp over the wreck.
> Night roared, with the heart-break hearing a heart-broke rabble,
> The woman's wailing, the crying of child without check –
> Till a lioness arose breasting the babble,
> A prophetess towered in the tumult, a virginal tongue told.

Here, not in Milton, is the vision of evil and restoration of the blissful seat. Small wonder that Hopkins 'admired' Milton, and 'did otherwise'.

That is the way Aurobindo works, starting from that magnificent first line in which poetry is profound revelation: "It was the hour before the gods awake", constituting a very Indian recognition of the *Brahmimuhurta*, an auspicious moment purged of "the fury and the mire of human veins" and looking forward to the resplendent dawn or Usha: what is *sobha*, beautiful to the eye, must be *subha*, auspicious to the mind and heart. This being a very significant recognition by an Indian poet who draws attention in literature to a concept much observed in life – at birth, death, marriage, naming of the child, housewarming, even such routine things as departure from home and arrival and in every undertaking – but which is conspicuous by its absence in literary criticism!

Constant prattling about the "vision of Evil" must make no sense to a people who perceive at once the fullness *(purnam)* behind the apparent nothingness, hence "the fathomless zero". What child's play is a reading of the Miltonic passage in which words mean but one thing and one thing only without the *rasagati*, the flow of rasa in the manner of enactment. This to me marks a refreshing departure from the orotundity of Milton's opening lines tumbling down breathlessly, while in Aurobindo the enactment is in terms of images, very different from the simple narrative statement of Milton as we see in:

> Across the path of the Divine Event
> The huge foreboding mind of night alone
> in her unlit temple of eternity
> Lay stretched immobile upon silence's marge
> Almost, one felt opaque, impenetrable
> In the sombre symbol of her eyeless Muse

The abysm of the unbodied infinite
A fathomless zero occupied the world.

The negatives "across", "foreboding", "unlit", "immobile" stand out
in their imagistic embodiment until they are interrupted by the unpoetical
"Almost" in the attempt to shift the focus from the object to the subject,
from the Night to one's own self, to give us recognition of Man's place
and plight in relation to the Night, which is again followed by a series of
negative images: "impenetrable", "eyeless", "abysm" and "unbodied" with
the culminating line: 'A fathomless zero occupied the world'.

If the "unlit temple" raises in us hopes of the possibility of an earnest
pilgrim kindling light and illuminating it, this is a far cry from the
svabhavokti of Milton. The light hidden by the encircling gloom must be
earned the hard way. Indeed, the insistence on negatives sums up the anguished wanderings of Aswapathi in the dark world until he comes to the
presence of light, the beatitude, or *sakshatkara*. The fathomless zero, which
is *sunya*, charged with rich ambiguity, in the sense of nothing to all ap-
pearances, and *purna*, or fullness to the perceiving eye, can only be puz-
zled out by an insider to the Upanishadic tradition, or one who has earned
access to it. Here, not in I.A. Richards, is the "Meaning of Meaning"!

Let us turn now to Raja Rao, the author of *Kanthapura*, then a young
man of 26 living in France with his French wife and writing about the
Indian national movement as it affected a tiny village called Kanthapura
in the interior of Mysore. Here is the "Novelist as Teacher", to borrow
Achebe's phrase, and this is the way Rao seeks to inculcate a sense of tradition in fictional terms:

> Cornerhouse Narasamma's son Moorthy was going through our
> backyard one day and seeing a half-sunk linga, said: "why not unearth it
> and wash it and consecrate it?" [Here is the immemorial India which
> invested every rock and tree and water place with divinity]. "Why not?"
> said we all and as it was the holidays and all the city boys were in the
> village, they began to put up a little mud wall and the tile roof to protect
> the god.

The stone has ceased to be dull inert matter. It assumes a personality
and acquires an aesthetic appeal when we learn "He was so big and fine
and brilliant". Aesthetics was never divorced from religion in this culture,
hence the "consecration ceremony" for the stone by Bhatta, the village
priest. And religion in turn fertilizes social life as in what follows:

Rangamma said she would pay for the milk and banana libation and a dinner; we had a grand feast. Then came postmaster Suryanarayana and said "Brother, why not start a Sankara Jayanthi? I have the texts; we shall read the Sankara Vijaya and somebody will offer a dinner for each day of the month". "Let the first be mine", said Bhatta. "The second mine", insisted Pandit Venkateshiah. "And the fourth and the fifth are mine", said Rangamma. "And if nobody is coming forward for the other days, let it always be mine".

It is not only that Raja Rao succeeds in writing a classic on a village but that he does so employing the dialect of the village, its spirit so beautifully preserved in the English rendering. Religion, we have seen, made for a feeling of a close-knit community. And this is still the pattern as we see celebrations of the Ganesha festival and Sriramanavami at the street corners of our urban centres, Delhi, Bombay, Calcutta not excluding.

Now for a sample of how sophisticated science and the application of science come to the village through small-town newspapers such as *Visvakarnataka*, *Desabandhu* and *Jayakarnataka*, newspapers sneered at then as now as "three pice rags" but which suffice to educate the villager as learned books may not: Jagadish Chandra Bose's discovery of "the plants that weep", Darwin's Theory of Evolution in "the monkeys that were the men we have become"; modern researches in germ theory as "the worms thin as dust that get into your blood and give you dysentery and plague and cholera". Sir James Jeans' "Mysterious Universe" comes to Rangamma with a minimum of simplicity but also a sense of humour as: "the stars that are so far that some have poured their light into the blue space long before you were born or your father was born and your grandfather was born". And consider, finally, how a stern scientific truth is absorbed into a rich unified sensibility: "out there (the telescope) there is just a chink and you put your eyes to a great life and see another world with sun and moon and stars, all bright and floating in the diamond dust of God".

Kanthapura cannot be classified as a historical or political novel. It is a work of art with a keen sense of the age in which it was written, with timeless truths enacted within the framework of time. While Raja Rao seems to be very much on the side of Gandhi in the novel, he does not fail to frown on the betrayal of the poor and the helpless as the novel closes with references to Range Gowda, who had been "a tiger to the authorities" but who is now "lean as an areca", and to Chinna, "lifting her leg" to her patrons for a living. Moorthy, who was at the centre of the movement, has sunk into anonymity and the village has been reduced to roofless, doorless houses with "neither man nor mosquito" to be seen. It is easy for a writer handling political themes to be lost on the side of the slogan-shouters who made commotion possible, but he must, as a man of vision, anticipate the fatal errors of hot-headed revolutionaries and suggest correctives to the emergence of a Caesar or a Napoleon. *Kanthapura* concludes in the manner of our great epics, with a teasing quality:

Is this the reward for the brave and the suffering, or the innocent?

But what resides with us finally is an impression of the heroic and noble heights to which the ordinary man can rise, the extraordinary behind the ordinary, the truth of a democratic age and the vitality of a great tradition, not the ignoble, unedifying whining in pity and fear. The final note, despite "the heart it beat like a drum", is one of *Shantha*, stasis, which at first eluded Ignatio Silone of *Fontamara*, written to protest against Mussolini's misrule and which provides creative parallels to Raja Rao's *Kanthapura*.

I have only cited two examples from Indian English Writing of the contemporary scene to suggest that a national literature has been taking shape, connecting it with the life and literature of the past of India and absorbing influences from the modern West on its own terms, which is to say without losing its identity. Similar tendencies can perhaps be discerned in some regional works too, though one fears that the tendency is to let Western modes and values supplant traditional Indian values in the interest of modernity, which obviously is a trend in the wrong direction and inimical to the growth of a national literature.

INDEPENDENCE, NATIONALISM & THE RUSH OF ETERNITY IN THE MALGUDI CHRONICLES

SYD HARREX
Flinders University of South Australia

Inevitably, Indo-British relationships have provided one of the major themes in fiction set in India. The novels, short stories, autobiographies and literary prose written in English belong to two distinct, though not necessarily mutually exclusive traditions. One is the 'Anglo-Indian', represented by such figures as Kipling, Thompson, Forster and Scott and defined according to the old Raj use of the term. Strictly speaking this literary tradition is non-Indian, but the boundary signified by the hyphen in the word is blurred not just by 'colonial discourse' and 'ambivalence' *per se,* but by the writers' attitudes and practises in relation to the cultural phenomena signified by these latter-day terms.

The main tradition in English, of course, is the Indian-English which, as generations of Indian critics of this literature have declared, has legitimate claims to national status on the grounds of language, achievement and pan-Indian provenance. It is defined by, as well as linguistic practice, citizenship and identity, particularly as perceived by individual writers in relation to their own origins; its ranks accordingly include Eurasian Indians as well as – somewhat problematically of late – expatriates, particularly novelists.

A further generalisation I begin with is that Indian-English writers of fiction, in presenting the Indo-British relationship, have focused intensely and pervasively on the independence struggle, partition, and the political aftermath, thereby imbuing the social textures of their narratives with a wide range of interconnected political, economic and cultural issues, problems and conflicts. While the older generation of twentieth-century novelists – Mulk Raj Anand, R. K. Narayan and Raja Rao – began fictionalising their impressions of Raj colonialism 15 years before independence, the next generation of fiction-writers portrayed and interrogated this history with such commitment that they were in effect establishing their post-colonial and post-independence credentials. Their debt to the pioneering work of Anand, Raja Rao and Narayan was significant, as it also was to such national figures as Rabindranath Tagore and Premchand.

The first Indian-English classic of Independent India emerged in 1948, G.V. Desani's *All About H. Hatterr,* a fantastic celebration and satire of mimicry, hybridity and ambivalence; a pre-emptive post-modernist exploration of post-coloniality. In the preface to the novel its author tells us he wrote it in London sitting in the front row of World War II. A British BBC colleague was not impressed, reprimanding him for writing fiction when his energies should have been devoted to the war effort. That colleague, in the role of superior officer disciplining the subaltern, was George Orwell.

The turmoil and conflicts agitating Indo-British relationships, captured in novel after novel, did not extend, however, to Indian-English attitudes to the English language, English literature and British writers. Anand's first novel *Untouchable* (1935) was published as a result of E.M. Forster agreeing to write a preface; Narayan's first, *Swami and Friends*, also published in 1935, owed its publication to the supportive influence of Graham Greene. Forster commended the Indianness of Anand's presentation of his distasteful subject, while Greene was enchanted by a distinctive fictional world which had never before been encountered in English fiction. Greene claimed to have found an Indian Chekhov.

While millions of readers in the major languages were discovering their country's past and present histories in political narratives, the writers and their advocates interpreted this literary nationalism as a revolutionary displacement of the hegemonic colonial discourse. Anand vigorously attacked – as the main sources of oppression – caste, religion, colonialism, imperialism, corruption, privilege, poverty and so on. Raja Rao created a new art form, merging oral narrative and culturally-laden Indian-English dialect, to transcreate the dynamics of Gandhiism, the politics of moral force, the mobilisation of peaceful protest, and the suffering and nobility of a fallible people.

What then was Narayan's response in his fiction to the culture of colonialism and the Raj's colonialist discourses? We get some idea from his fourth novel *The English Teacher,* a quasi-autobiography published two years prior to India's "tryst with destiny". It was produced out of personal painful circumstances – the death of Narayan's wife – that almost put an end to his writing career. I want to return your attention to some much quoted statements made by the narrator-persona, Krishnan, concerning his decision to resign from his financially-secure college lectureship. Krishnan plans a letter of resignation for which he has high hopes as a counteractive discourse and manifesto:

> I would send in a letter which would be a classic in its own way, and which would singe the fingers of whoever touched it. In it I was going to attack a whole century of false education. I was going to explain why I could no longer stuff Shakespeare and Elizabethan metre and Romantic poetry for the hundredth time into young minds and feed them on the dead mutton of literary analysis and theories and histories, while what they needed was lessons in the fullest use of the mind. This education had reduced us to a nation of morons; we were strangers to our own culture and camp followers of another culture, feeding on leavings and garbage. (205)

But after filling three sheets which amount to a belated writing back to Macaulay's Minute on Education, Krishnan passes a judgement of immaturity upon himself, a judgement against his "theatrical and pompous" (206) "rehash of an article entitled 'Problems of Higher Education' " (206). "I was entangled too much in theories and platitudes", he acknowledges: "It was like a rabid attack on all English writers, which was hardly my purpose." (206) We detect in Krishnan a glimmering realisation that the cause of independence is not achieved by empty rhetoric, irrelevant attitudes, and inflated passion. Moreover, his legitimate critique of the English system of education, apparently at odds with his legitimate (personally rewarding) love of English literature, gives rise to a positive ambivalence which prompts him to ask a crucial question: "What about our own roots?" (206) With this question Krishnan arrives at a doorstep of self-knowledge which begins with his statement to himself, "There is something far deeper that I wish to say." (179)

The ending of the novel suggests that the "something far deeper" is in the order of an Indian spiritual acceptance which no colonial discourse could presume to provide. All this implies, I think, that Narayan makes Krishnan's development a declaration of personal independence which anticipates India's political independence as an achievement created from Indian resources of self-worth and identity, and the repudiation of colonialism as an offence against a people's rights and dignity. Krishnan's reanimated idealism coincides in historical time, appropriately, with the climactic achievements of Gandhi's political idealism, and Krishnan's new life as a responsible father and community worker resonates with the potentialities of the imminent new India.

Narayan's approach to weighty national concerns in his fictions of daily life tend, however, to be wryly sceptical of high expectations, purity of motive, and unity of purpose. As the chronicler of Malgudi, Narayan creates a local history which is located in the social interactions and the psyches of his Malgudian characters, many of whom, by their reappearances in novels and short stories over decades, contribute a sense of cultural continuity to Narayan's microcosm of South India. In the comic and cautionary chronicles of Malgudi, history emerges as anecdote, fragmentary chronology, a collage of architectural and behavioural mannerisms, and myth-informed memory. Although Malgudi is an open and public place subject to the diversifying influences of colonialism, nationalist politics and post-coloniality, subject to chaotic administrative bureaucracies, it is also a society with its own stable core of coherent archetypes. Typically, Narayan's narrative endings affirm the abiding presence of a collective centre where positive possibilities of meaning or enlightenment, acceptance or predetermined resolution, may be found.

Narayan is an astute and dedicated observer who exposes the politics of personal and social behaviour through the apparently vicarious curiosity and compassionate disinterest of the invisible storyteller. As a popular humorist, like his brother the cartoonist R.K. Laxman, Narayan's journalism dissolves the boundaries between comedy, caricature and satire. Typical targets are amalgamated in the spectacle of an absurdist bureaucracy implementing a supposedly democratic government programme for national integration which results in cultural totalitarianism. An example of Narayan's satirical treatment of this kind of obsession is "Government Music" (Next Sunday, 1956) in which he employs a simplified version of Swift's ironic rhetoric of rationality:

> The nation's musical policy will, needless to say, bear the colour and stamp of the minister holding the portfolio. He may decree that a Fifty-five year plan for the musical revival and integration of the country... should be taken up immediately. In order to facilitate the integration of north and south, it will be suggested that a South Indian audience should sit through a performance of North Indian music for a minimum of twelve hours each quarter, and vice-versa. And the audience must show no boredom or weariness. Any sign of restlessness will be viewed as an unnational activity. Yawning at such a function will be punishable with both fine and reprimand. Looking about for an exit will be interpreted

as a lack of interest in the performance; the burden of proving otherwise will be on the man so charged. In every music *sabha* there will be
a government-appointed watch-and-ward inspector with a staff com-
mensurate with the strength of the *sabha*. His business will be to keep
an eye on the audience and see that people do not nod... he will be quite
entitled to switch off the microphone of the singer and switch on his
own microphone, which he will always keep cleverly concealed on his
person, and cry, preferably in a musical manner, "Wake up citizens, this
is not the time to sleep" (16-17).

This government paper concludes with an exhortation to composers
who celebrate love and devotion to also "compose songs that will give our
villagers... an incentive to try the Japanese method of rice cultivation,
conserve topsoil, and mend their own roads and drains without waiting
for government help". (19)
   Narayan casts a cold eye on political correctness long before this term
became a political target. "Street Names", an essay for his Sunday column in *The Times of India,* begins with the statement, "In the India of
post-1947, the most marked feature is the passion for changing names
of streets, towns, parks and squares" *(Next Sunday,*211). Narayan argues
that citizens don't know or care about whomever a street is named after,
their only concern being the security of familiarity with which they find
their 'way about the town'. Narayan rests his case with an appeal to
Gandhian doctrine:

> *Ahimsa,* the essence of which is that we should not hate our enemies,
> much less our dead enemies... the despot's name should be left un-
> touched just to show his despotism has proved futile in the long run.
> Acrimony, contemporaneous or in retrospect, can have no place in a
> nation nurtured on *Ahimsa.* And will you remember, you passionate
> changer of street names, the tradition thus started by you may be con-
> tinued by someone else coming to your place later, whose views may
> be different from yours? (214)

Narayan addresses this patriotic phenomenon comically and satirically
in "Lawley Road", one of his Talkative Man monologues. In this story
the Municipal Chairman of Malgudi, who had made his fortune "as a
supplier of blankets to the army during the War" (7) and thereby bought
his public office, enhances his power and prestige by riding the tide of
independence jubilation and patriotism. But these gratifications soon
abate and he seeks more enduring ways of glorifying his image, first by

transforming the directory of place names and next by removing the statue of Sir Frederick Lawley who, according to Council research, was the most vicious and tyrannical of colonisers:

> People dropped their normal occupations and loitered around the statue, wondering how they could have tolerated it for so many years. The gentleman seemed to smile derisively at the nation now, with his arms locked behind and sword dangling from his belt. There could be no doubt that he must have been the worst tyrant imaginable: the true picture – with breeches and wig and white waistcoat and that hard determined look – of all that has been hatefully familiar in the British period of Indian history (9-10).

Both the Chairman's projects, however, turn into fiascos. There comes a point when, the Talkative Man says, "the Council just went mad. It decided to give the same name to four different streets... letters went where they were not wanted, people were not able to say where they lived or direct others there" (8-9). Then the removal of the Lawley statue, accompanied by fervent press publicity, is exposed as a blunder of national magnitude, for the Lawley commemorated in the Malgudi statue was a different personage altogether to the one the Council was obliterating from historical memory: a benevolent progressive administrator who foreshadowed Home Rule and died "in the great Sarayu floods while attempting to save the lives of villagers along its banks" (12). When the Government threatens to dissolve the Council because of its, shall we say, monumental blunder, the Chairman has to buy back the statue and acquire a property for its permanent location – all at his own expense – to retain office. This satiric and ironic reversal, or poetic justice, is a pattern underlying many of Narayan's stories and episodes in his novels. It is repeated, for example, in *Waiting for the Mahatma* (1955), in the Malgudi Municipal Chairman's fatal attempts to ingratiate himself with Gandhi and promote the Mahatma's visit as a political and administrative triumph for himself.

Any consideration of Narayan's post-Independence portrayal of Gandhi and his legacy has to begin with *Waiting for the Mahatma* in which the portrait of Gandhi is not a focal point for the narration of epic events, but a counterpoint for a love story: Sriram's gauche and desperate wooing of Bharati. This makes for occasional intimate engagements with Gandhi who is presented in a series of close-ups from the eyewitness vantage points of Bharati as well as of Sriram when he listens to Gandhi's speeches, is admitted into the Mahatma's presence, and becomes a member of Gandhi's entourage. Other close-ups are provided courtesy of the omniscient novelist's satiric perspectives on politics and egomania.

Memorable examples of the latter appear in such scenes as the Reception Committee's meeting in preparation for Gandhi's visit, Municipal Chairman Natesh's inaudible welcome speech, and Gandhi's rejection of Natesh's palatial accommodation in favour of a hut in the untouchable colony:

> His arguments as to why he alone should be Mahatmaji's host seemed unassailable: "I have spent two lakhs on the building, my garden and lawns alone have cost me twenty-five thousand rupees so far. What do you think I have done it for? I am a simple man, sir, my needs are very simple. I don't need any luxury. I can live in a hut, but the reason I have built it on this scale is so that I should be able for at least once in my lifetime to receive a great soul like Mahatmaji. This is the only house in which he can stay comfortably when he comes to this town. Let me say without appearing to be boastful that it is the biggest and the best furnished house in Malgudi, and we as the people of Malgudi have a responsibility to give him our very best, so how can we house him in any lesser place?"
>
> The Reception Committee applauded his speech. The District Collector, who was the head of the district, and the District Superintendent of Police, who was next to him in authority, attended the meeting as *ex-officio* members.
>
> A dissenting voice said, "Why not give the Circuit House for Mahatmaji?"
>
> The Circuit House on the edge of the town was an old East India Company building standing on an acre of land, on the Trunk Road. Robert Clive was supposed to have halted there while marching to relieve the siege of Trichinopoly. The citizens of Malgudi were very proud of this building and never missed an opportunity to show it off to anyone visiting the town and it always housed the distinguished visitors who came this way. It was a matter of prestige for Governors to be put up there. Even in this remote spot they had arranged to have all their conveniences undiminished with resplendent sanitary fittings in the bathrooms. It was also known as the Glass House, by virtue of a glass-fronted bay room from which the distinguished guests could watch the wild animals that were supposed to stray near the building at night in those days.
>
> The dissenting voice in the Reception Committee said, "Is it the privilege of the ruling race alone to be given the Circuit House? Is our Mahatmaji unworthy of it?"

The Collector, who was the custodian of British prestige, rose to a point of order and administered a gentle reproof to the man who spoke:
"It is not good to go beyond the relevant facts at the moment: If we have considered the Circuit House as unsuitable it is because we have no time to rig it up for receiving Mr Gandhi."
It was a point of professional honour for him to say Mr Gandhi and not *Mahatma,* and but for the fact that as the Collector he could close the entire meeting and put all the members behind bars under the Defence of India Act, many would have protested and walked out, but they held their peace and he drove home the point.
"Since Mr Gandhi's arrival has been a sudden decision, we are naturally unable to get the building ready for him; if I may say so, our chairman's house seems to suit the purpose and we must be grateful to him for so kindly obliging us."
"And I am arranging to move to the Glass House leaving my house for Mahatmaji's occupation."
That seemed to decide it, and his partisans cheered loudly.

Having so deftly satirised the pretensions of the Municipal Chairman and the hauteur of the colonial administrator, Narayan effortlessly amplifies the attack in relation to the Chairman's "address of welcome":

He had spent a whole week composing the text of the address with the help of a local journalist, adding whatever would show off either his patriotism or the eminent position Malgudi occupied in the country's life. The Collector had taken the trouble to go through the address before it was sent for printing in order to make sure that it contained no insult to the British Empire, that it did not hinder the war effort, and that it in no way betrayed military secrets. He had to censor it in several places: where the Chairman compared Malgudi to Switzerland... a reference to the hosiery trade... this was a blatant advertisement for the Chairman's goods... and all those passages which hinted at the work done by Gandhiji in the political field. The picture of him as a social reformer was left intact and even enlarged; anyone who read the address would conclude that politics were the last thing that Mahatmaji was interested in. (26)

The amusing satiric parody here is neatly counterpointed by the genuine affectionate respect for Gandhi implicit in the references to him as 'Gandhiji' and 'Mahatmaji'.
The novel's opening, with Gandhi's imminent visit high on the agenda, provides for the forthcoming narrative a time and truth frame exhibited

in the two following statements:

> Sriram suddenly came out of an age-old somnolence, and woke to the
> fact that Malgudi was about to have the honour of receiving Mahatma
> Gandhi. (14)

> Some people conveniently adopt patriotism when Mahatmaji arrives. (16)

The historical sense of period is refracted through incidental reference
to Gandhi's resistance to the British as well as by some traumatic effects of
the Independence Struggle on the personal histories of some of the characters. Bharati's father died during the 1920 Satyagraha campaign, her
mother died soon after, and she was adopted by the local Sevat Sangh and
given her name meaning Daughter of India. As the disciple Gorpad explains to Sriram:

> "That was during the first non-cooperation days in 1920; her father
> led the first batch of *Satyagrahis* who were going to take down the Union
> Jack from the Secretariat at Madras. He was beaten with a police lathi
> and a blow fell on his chest and he dropped dead, but my father was
> shot.... He was picketing a shop where they were selling toddy and other
> alcoholic drinks, and a police company came and asked him to go away,
> but he refused. A crowd gathered, and there was a lot of mess and in the
> end the police shot him point blank." He wiped away tears at the memory
> of it. "I will not rest till the British are sent out of India," his voice was
> thick with sorrow. "My brother became a terrorist and shot dead many
> English officials, nobody knows his whereabouts. I should also have
> joined him and shot many more Englishmen, but our Mahatma will not
> let me be violent even in thought," he said ruefully.
>   Sriram wishing to sound very sympathetic said, "All Englishmen de-
> serve to be shot. They have been very cruel."
>   "You should not even think on those lines, if you are going to be a true
> *Satyagrahi*," said the other. (50)

Narayan introduces references to the effects of World War II on India
with respect to famine and grain-hoarding, the subversive activities of
Subhas Chandra Bose, and Gandhi's imprisonment following his Quit
India resolution:

> The Mahatma had in his famous resolution of August 1942 said: "Brit-
> ain must quit India," and the phrase had the potency of a mantra or a

magic formula. Throughout the length and breadth of the land, people cried "Quit India." The Home Secretary grew uneasy at the sound of it. It became a prohibited phrase in polite society. After the Mahatma uttered the phrase, he was put in prison; but the phrase took life and flourished, and did ultimately produce enough power to send the British out. There was not a blank wall in the whole of the country which did not carry the message. Wherever one turned one saw "Quit India" (68).

This overview is counterpointed by a scene in which the logic of Sriram's sign-painting is challenged:

> In one place a man asked Sriram: "What is the use of your writing 'Quit India' in all these places. Do you want us to quit?"
> "It does not mean that."
> "Then write it where it can be seen by those to whom it is meant."
> (73)

And it has to be said that Sriram's subversive, pseudo-terrorist activities are petty, insignificant and ultimately embarrassing as his prison reflections make clear:

> He was amazed at the isolation that had been devised... He had lost count of time... He was losing his identity. He had lost his patriotic aim. He wondered what he had done to warrant anyone calling him a political sufferer. But for Jagadish he would not have done things that he wouldn't wish to enumerate.before any decent person now. (135)

This must be construed as a measure of Sriram's failure to adhere to Gandhi's principles and good counsel. When a friendly warder smuggles in a newspaper, Sriram (and the reader) finally catches up with the political timetable – impending partition, the 'Mahatma's firm refusal to countenance the proposal,' the 'cabinet Mission', 'death, disaster, and convulsive changes'. Narayan comments ironically that "The greatest triumph for Sriram was that the British were definitely quitting India. He said proudly, 'I wrote on all the walls "Quit India", and you see it has taken effect'." (145)

However, Sriram's adjustment to his twofold freedom – liberated from prison into Independent India – begins with a phase of psychological and social insecurity which only dissipates when he is reunited with Bharati in Delhi where Gandhi gives them his blessing for their marriage immediately before he goes, with premonitions of his death, to meet his assassin's bullets. The novel ends with the finality of the assassination.

During the course of the narrative Narayan does much more than pay lip-service to Gandhi's charisma, philosophy, discipline and leadership. The Mahatma is framed within the smaller-scale concerns of ordinary realities – of the untouchables, the youth, the self-interested bourgeoisie, social impurities – and resists the veneration and adoration of his person. His adherence to and espousal of 'discipline' receives a lot of narrative emphasis; particularly "Ram Dhun: spinning on the charka and the practice of absolute Truth and Nonviolence" (17). Bharati tells Sriram, "in Bapu's presence we speak only the absolute truth" (47). Narayan sketches a classical picture of Gandhi's pilgrimage to the people:

> Gandhiji's personal life went on as if he had been stationary in one place; the others adjusted themselves to it. He met the local village men and women, spoke to them about God, comforted the ailing, advised those who sought his guidance. He spoke to them about spinning, the war, Britain, and religion.... He trudged his way through ploughed fields, he climbed hard rocky places, through mud and slush, but always with the happiest look, and no place seemed too small for his attentions (60).

Out of the mouth Narayan has given him, Gandhi's essential messages are embedded in the text:

> "I want you really to make sure of a change in your hearts before you think of asking the British to leave the shores of India... I want you to clear your hearts and minds and make certain that only love resides there, and there is no residue of bitterness for past history. Only then can you say to the British, "Please leave this country to be managed or mismanaged by us, that's purely our own business, and come back any time you like as our friend and distinguished guest, not as our rulers,' and you will find John Bull packing his suitcase. But be sure you have love in your heart and not bitterness... If I have the slightest suspicion that your heart is not pure or that there is bitterness there, I'd rather have the British stay on. It's the lesser of two evils" (19-20).

This puritan doctrine is spelled out in sufficient detail to ensure that *Waiting for the Mahatma* is approvingly encoded with Gandhi's sincerity. On another occasion Narayan's Gandhi says: "You must train yourself to become a hundred per cent *ahimsa* soldier. You must become so sensitive that it is not possible for you to wear sandals made of the hide of slaughtered animals" (52).

Sriram is a representative of the human norm who, though inspired by

Gandhi's teaching, finds it difficult to consistently live up to it in practice. He signifies the young dormant consciousness existing in a cosy state of apathy until stirred into moral awareness by Gandhi's big-picture messages. He also represents in his ulterior motive – his romantic infatuation for Bharati – those normal people who brought to the freedom movement, along with their self-sacrifice and dedication, their personal egos and ambitions. Sriram's innocence and romanticism serve as antidotes to any novelistic temptation to sentimentalise and romanticise Gandhi and the independence struggle. Narayan frames the history with an ironic surveillance that precludes naive·and fanciful illusions about human behaviour, yet distils an essence of Gandhi's principles, power, and leadership, his commitment to a humanist moral order. Particularly in his use of tone and relief the novelist reverences the man of history.

The ending of *Waiting for the Mahatma* was predetermined; in this case fact was superior to fiction. Gandhi celebrated independence in Calcutta, attempting to curb the blood-letting. "He said that if a country cannot give security to women and children, it is not worth living in" (165). In Delhi, fostering the orphans of communal violence is Bharati's vocation. Gandhi's pronouncements and actions, and Bharati's devotion, determine the moral sway in *Waiting for the Mahatma,* a novel in which Gandhi's life and achievements are modestly celebrated and in which his death is frozen in time.

Narayan's perspective on modern Indian history in *Waiting for the Mahatma* is firmly located within micro-historical experience. His later psychological studies – as in *The Sweet-Vendor* and *A Tiger for Malgudi* for instance – are of characters whose ultimate decisions about selfhood are influenced by traditional values derived in part from the Gandhian ethical system. Retreat from the world is a rite of passage from the micro-historical reality to a macro-historical existentialism. Jagan, the sweet-vendor and Gandhi disciple, finds that the only just way to escape the excessive demands of his unorthodox son, and an embarrassing domestic situation, is a pragmatic renunciation of his home-and-business life. When Jagan meets an eccentric mystic who persuades him to buy a garden-retreat and install a goddess there, he finds 'it was difficult... to believe that he was in the twentieth century... The edge of reality itself was beginning to blur; this man from the previous millennium seemed to be the only object worth notice' (118). Flowing from this experience are Jagan's conscious articulations of his new sense of selfhood:

"God knows I need a retreat. You know, my friend, at some stage in one's life one must uproot oneself from the accustomed surroundings and disappear so that others may continue in peace."

"It would be the most accredited procedure according to our scriptures – husband and wife must vanish into the forest at some stage in their lives, leaving the affairs of the world to younger people." (126)

At the latter extremity of the Indian spectrum, spanning from the micro- to the macro-historical, is Narayan's vision of life and history as physical and metaphysical palimpsest, momentarily visible on the microscopic 'screen':

Srinivas suddenly said to himself: "I might be in the twentieth century B.C. for all it matters...." His scenario-writing habit suddenly asserted itself... Malgudi itself dimmed and dissolved... Presently appeared... Sri Rama. ... the Buddha... Shankara... the Christian missionary... Edward Shilling and his Englandia Bank... Dynasties rose and fell. "What did it amount to?" Srinivas asked himself as the historical picture faded out... in the rush of eternity nothing mattered. *(Mr. Sampath,* 208)

REFERENCES

Harrex S. C., *The Fire and the Offering: the English language Novel of India 1935-1970,* Calcutta: Writers Workshop. Vol. 1 1977, Vol.2. 1978.
Narayan, R. K., *Lawley Road And Other Stories,* Delhi: Hind Pocket Books (Orient Paperbacks). n.d.
——, *Next Sunday,* Mysore: Indian Thought Publications, 1956.
——, *The English Teacher,* Mysore: Indian Thought Publications, 1968.
——, *The Sweet Vendor,* London: The Bodley Head, 1967.
——, *Mr. Sampath,* Mysore: Indian Thought Publications, 1971
——, *Waiting for the Mahatma,* Mysore: Indian Thought Publications, 1976

A LITERARY VOYAGE TO INDIA :
ROHINTON MISTRY'S *A FINE BALANCE*

SAVITA GOEL
University of Jaipur

The endeavour to write a novel about one's native country on the basis of memory has been an irresistible challenge and a compelling necessity for a number of exiled or immigrant writers who have been cut off from their native roots. Their backward glance home conceals their desire for their lost home and their "criticism of the reality of home reaffirms the same longing, though in an inverted manner" (Kirpal, 6). Salman Rushdie, too, in *Imaginary Homelands* contends that "writers in my position, exiles or emigrants or expatriates, are haunted by some sense of loss, some urge to reclaim, to look back, even at the risk of being mutated into pillars of salt" (10). The act of expatriation may result in the loss of "first hand knowledge of economic, political, social changes, of current jargon, of debate, even of such geographic elements as landscape, climate and even vegetation" (Parameswaran, 43) and it seems that the expatriate writer has to work harder than the 'native' writer to create authenticity. Any writer who writes about his homeland from the outside must necessarily "deal in broken mirrors, some of whose fragments have been irretrievably lost" (Rushdie, 11). Nonetheless, it is precisely the fragmentary nature of these memories, the incomplete truths they contain, the partial explanations they offer, that make them particularly evocative for the transplanted writer. For Rushdie, these "shards of memory acquired greater status, greater resonance, because they were remains; fragmentation made trivial things seem like symbols, and the mundane acquired numinous qualities" (12).

Canada-based, Indian (Parsi) writer Rohinton Mistry's literary voyage continues to bring him to India. In his latest novel, *A Fine Balance* (winner of the prestigious Commonwealth Writers Prize, 1996), which is reminiscent of his earlier works – *Tales from Firozsha Baag* and *Such A Long*

Journey, he again tries to revise the history of his homeland, his community and family. In this he reveals his diasporic consciousness. But there is no nostalgia in Mistry's backward glance. He writes with all the authenticity of the insider, but the distance of Canada lends his writing an outsider's objectivity. The present paper discusses Mistry's perspective on the political and social chaos underlying India's colonial and post-colonial experience. *A Fine Balance*, set in Indira Gandhi's India, and more specifically during the time of the Emergency, is a stark and moving portrait of life during this period. It reflects the reality of India – the predatory politics of corruption, tyranny, exploitation, violence and bloodshed. The paper also focuses in particular on Mistry's portrayal of rural India and his depiction of India's traumas along communal, religious and linguistic fault-lines.

At the same time as dealing with the lives of common people in post-independent India, the novel captures the socio-political-cultural turmoil of this period. Mistry achieves the feat of mixing a broad historical span with his close focus on his characters's personal lives. Specifically, he attempts to portray the reality of India by weaving together four different worlds in the fabric of the novel. The first is the middle class, urban world of Dina Dalal, a pretty widow in her forties. Then there is a glimpse into the rural India provided by Ishvar Darji and his nephew – Omprakash – chamars who attempt to liberate themselves from caste stereotypes by becoming tailors in Bombay, but who gradually get caught in the quagmire of Bombay's underworld. There is another world symbolized by Maneck Kohlah, a sensitive Parsi boy, whose activities bring the reader into the world of the university student. The novel is as much about the shared lives of these four major characters, who at one stage live under the same roof, as it is about their separate entities.

Mistry's pessimistic image of his motherland is conveyed most acutely in his depiction of the atrocities committed on the untouchables, the chamars who spend their life in obedient compliance with the traditions of the caste system and survive only with humiliation and forbearance as their constant companions. When they attempt to resist, their punishments are merciless. When Buddhu's wife refuses to go to the field with the zamindar's son, her head is shaved and she is forced to walk naked through the square. Dukhi's wife is raped. They are trapped in a world where any unwary action can result in punishment. Their so-called 'crimes' include those of a Bhungi who dares to let his unclean eyes meet a Brahmin's eyes; a chamar who has walked on the wrong side of the temple road and defiled it; another who has strayed near a puja and allowed his undeserving ears to overhear the sacred shlokas. The children of the low castes are denied the right to education so when Ishvar and Narayan dare to enter a schoolroom they are caned severely. When Narayan dares to assert his right to vote, he and his companions are hung naked by their ankles from the branches of a banyan tree and the thakur's men:

> Urinated on the three inverted faces. Semiconscious, the parched mouths were grateful for the moisture, licking the trickle with feeble urgency... burning coals were held to the three men's genitals, then stuffed into their mouths. Their screams were heard through the village until their lips and tongues melted away. (Mistry, 146)

Their bodies are displayed in the village square and their entire families burnt alive. Mistry focuses unblinkingly on man's inhumanity to man and on the deprivation and inequities faced by the underprivileged in India.

In Mistry's post-colonial India the plight of the common people has not improved and they have to face the same exploitation and injustice as under colonialism. As one character says, "Of course, for ordinary people, nothing has changed" (581). Native rulers have merely replaced foreign rulers and the Indian government has failed to resolve the basic problems of poverty, hunger, unemployment, illiteracy and disease. Indeed the gap between the rich and the poor has widened. The writer draws a pathetic picture of near-naked people in Bombay slums, with meagre possessions, and lean, emaciated babies, hungry and crying whom their parents feed with "half-rotten bananas and oranges and scraps scavenged the night before" (330). This wound in India's social body is depicted in individual images of chill penury:

> Outside the platform, a woman sat in the sun ... drying her laundered sari, one half at a time. One end was wound wet round her waist and over her shrunken breasts, as far as it would go. The drying half was stretched along the railway fence. (281)

Mistry "finds Bombay oppressive and overcrowded" (Mistry, Cyrus, 11). When he went back to Canada he told Hancock that Bombay had appeared very grim and bleak to him and that if the picture he created was bleak, "That's exactly the way it is" (148). He describes it this way:

> Eight, nine or ten people in a small room. Sleeping one over the other on big shelves, from floor to ceiling, like third-class railway berths. Or

in cupboards, or in the bathroom. Surviving like goods in a warehouse. (Mistry, 471)

The writer presents a cross-section of Bombay – the huge slum with its malodorous crown of cooking smoke and industrial effluvium, the long queues for water, accompanied by quarrels, open air toilets, the familiar sights of beggars and the beggarmaster paying the police every week to avoid harassment. Mistry's authentic portrayal of Bombay and its social ills bears a close affinity to Meera Nair's film *Salaam Bombay*. The description of the imaginative cunning of the beggarmaster, training his beggars and dressing them with a variety of wounds renders a grim kind of humour.

Demoralized by the ruthless murder of their entire family, pressured by joblessness and hunger and envisioning a bright future for themselves, the Chamars Ishvar and Omprakash migrate from the country to Bombay. They are like Rajaram who says, "thousands and thousands are coming to the city because of bad times in their native place. I came for the same reason" (171) and "the city grabs you, sinks its claws into you and refuses to let go" (172). In Bombay, like nomads, they move from Nawaz's awning to their slum dwelling, then to the railway platform and then to the entrance of a chemist's shop where they are mistaken for beggars, compelled to slog as labourers and finally released from this hell by the beggarmaster. Their inability to find a home, despite numerous efforts, is touching and pitiable. They are caught between two worlds: their native village, which they have had to abandon because of caste persecution, and Bombay, which has failed them despite its promises. They are marginal men, unable to discard the old and to find peace in the new.

Mistry deals with gender discrimination as another aspect of Indian reality, asserting that even within the hierarchy of poverty, Indian society confers higher status on men. Women are relegated to a subordinate status in family and society. They are expected to be dutiful daughters, loving mothers, submissive daughters-in-law and faithful wives. Patriarchy defines the narrow precincts women must keep to, where even a slight infringement of its boundaries is sufficient to arouse the wrath of its defenders. After marriage women become the property of their husbands to be abused and bullied. If daughters are born, women are thrashed by their husbands and ordered to discreetly get rid of the new born, who are strangled, poisoned or starved to death. When a son is born to Radha and Narayan, sweets are distributed and everyone rejoices with them. Shankar's mother has no nose because her drunken father slashed it off at birth because she is a daughter not a son. Avinash's three sisters, aware of their father's shame in not being able to afford dowries for them, commit suicide by hanging from a ceiling fan.

Earlier in her life, Dina, one of the main characters, is ill-treated by her brother, not allowed to visit her friends, made to do the household chores and polish his shoes. After Mrs. Shroff's death, despite her keen desire to pursue her education, Dina is not allowed to matriculate. Her brother tries to compel her to marry a person of his choice, but Dina asserts her individuality and marries Rustom Dalal, whom she loves intensely. Dina is a symbol of the "new woman" who refuses to be submissive and does not accept the stereotypical, feminine role assigned to her. Even on the cruel night when her husband dies, she behaves with dignified courage: "No wailing, no beating the chest or tearing the hair like you might expect from a woman who had suffered such a shock, such a loss" (46). She refuses to disintegrate and resolves to restructure her life to be economically independent of men. Her quest for selfhood and her emergence as a strong, progressive and independent woman forms the core of the novel. She it is who rescues the two tailors, Ishvar and Om, from the streets when she establishes Au Revoir Exports.

Through the world of Maneck and his friend Avinash, Mistry gives us a glimpse into the evils of Indian university life – the shameful ragging, the nepotism in hiring staff, the bribery for admissions, the sale of examination papers, the special privileges for politicians' families, government interference in the syllabus, intimidation of faculty members and the nature of student politics. Avinash's death remains a mystery, but the discovery of burns to his genitals suggest that he has not fallen off a train as claimed, but has been killed in police custody because of his involvement in student politics.

A Fine Balance views Indian society as decaying from top to bottom. Its leaders have exchanged wisdom and good governance for cowardice and self-aggrandisement. For votes and power they play with human lives and accept money from businessmen needing favours. Pre-election speeches are crammed with false promises, and for the politicians "passing laws is like passing water, it all ends down the drain" (143). Mistry lays bare the corruption of the election system of the world's largest democracy in which, for instance, illiterate villagers are cheated of their rights when their ballot papers are filled in by men hired by the politicians. Recalling the communal conflicts between Hindus and the Muslims at the time of Partition, Mistry faithfully describes the communal conflicts of 1984 caused by the death of Indira Gandhi, when Sikhs were ruthlessly burnt alive.

A Fine Balance, like Salman Rushdie's *Midnight's Children*, Nayantara Sahgal's *Rich Like Us* and Shashi Tharoor's *The Great Indian Novel* faithfully reflects the historical realities of the Emergency in India, when the world's largest democracy spent twenty-two months as the world's largest banana republic. In his stark and unsparing portrayal, every atrocity known to have been committed during the Emergency occurs to one or other of Mistry's characters. With the curtailing of the fundamental rights of the people, censorship of the press, imprisonment without trial and countless deaths in police custody, everything becomes topsy turvy. Valmik, the proof-reader, says, "I am inspired by the poet Yeats. I find his words relevant during this shameful Emergency – things fall apart, centre not holding, anarchy loosed upon the world" (556). Ishvar and Om suffer the most brutal aspect of the Emergency, when, among the poor, everyone, young or old, married or unmarried, was compelled to undergo a family planning operation. Om's testicles are removed just before his wedding and a botched operation results in the amputation of Ishvar's legs, turning both into crippled beggars.

The novel is not just a sordid drama of individual lives; it is also about the caring and sharing relationship that the four main characters gradually build up. There is Dina's kindly gestures in applying balm to Om's hand, and permitting the tailors to sleep on her verandah after their traumatic experience; there is Maneck neglecting his college course to help Dina to complete her dresses; there are the friendly moments they spend eating together, brightening their bleak lives. Maneck wishes that if "there were a large enough refrigerator, he would be able to preserve the happy times in this flat, keep them from ever spoiling" (440). Each of these characters encounter the challenges in their lives courageously. They have learnt to accept their fate and to make the best of it. As the proof-reader, Vasantrao Valmik, says, speaking it seems for Mistry: "the secret of survival is to embrace change and to adapt" (230), and he urges that one should learn to use one's failures as the stepping stones to success and that one has "to maintain a fine balance between hope and despair.... In the end, it's all a question of balance" (231). Though, in the end, Dina becomes dependent on her brother, she maintains a satisfying relationship with Ishvar and Om. At the end of the novel, now nearly blind, Dina sits with her two erstwhile tailors, now beggars, feeding them with massoor dal and chapatis, sharing memories of times past, closing the novel with warmth and the pleasure of sharing.

Beyond the four main characters, the book has a rich Dickensian cast of minor characters, such as the proof-reader Valmik, driven from his profession by a virulent allergy to printing ink to the new job of hiring crowds and shouting slogans in rallies, and the rent collector who cannot help smiling even though "his life had become the plot of a bad Hindi movie minus the happy ending" (90) and who at one point gives up: "It's no use. I cannot do this job, I hate it...". Besides these, there is Rajaram, who driven by extreme hunger changes from being a barber/hair-collector to becoming a Family Planning Motivator and then a murderer who kills two beggars for their lovely hair. Finally, he becomes the highly venerated saffron-clad Bal Baba whom superstitious Indian crowds queue to hear predict the future. He makes no charges, but announces that "all donations are mostly welcome by the Bal Bala Foundation, anymuch amount" (601). This is another facet of Indian reality.

In this novel, as in his earlier works, Mistry brings to the foreground the rich culture, customs and traditions of the marginalised Parsi community, and in scenes describing their death rites and funeral ceremonies he gives the reader a glimpse into the Parsi world. Figures such as the priest Dustoor Framji, known as Dustoor Daab-Chaab because of his propensity for squeezing young women, and Dina Dalal herself, with the innate kindness that sits on her form like her favourite blue dress, are totally convincing.

The Balzac quote at the beginning of the book, "this tragedy is not a fiction. All is true" seems to imply that Mistry wants the readers to read his account of the myriad lives that animate *A Fine Balance* as a faithful rendering of reality. However, whether his vision has the fine balance of the novel's title, or whether it is marked by pessimism and despair, each reader must decide.

REFERENCES

Hancock, Geoff, Interview with Rohinton Mistry, *The Canadian Fiction Magazine*, No.65. 1989: 143-150.

Kirpal, Viney, *The Third World Novel of Expatriation*, New Delhi: Sterling Publishers, 1989.

Mistry, Cyrus, *Sunday*, 27 Oct. 1991.

Mistry, Rohinton, *A Fine Balance*, New Delhi: Rupa and Co., 1996.

——, *Tales from Firozsha Baag*, London: Faber and Faber, 1987.

——, *Such a Long Journey*, Toronto: McClelland and Steward Inc., 1991.

Parameswaran, Uma, "What Price Expatriation?" *The Commonwealth Writer Overseas: Themes of Exile and Expatriation*, ed. Alastair Niven, Bruxelles: Libraire Marcel Didier, 1976.

Rushdie, Salman, *Imaginary Homelands*, London: Granta Books, 1991.

——, "The Free Radio," *East West*, London: Vintage, 1995.

——, *Midnight's Children* (1980), New York: Avon Books, 1982.

Sahgal, Nayantara, *Rich Like Us* (1985), London: Sceptre Edition, 1993.

Tharoor, Sashi, *The Great Indian Novel*, London: Picador, 1989.

III

INDIANS ABROAD

FROM INDIA TO CANADA VIA AFRICA:
M.G. VASSANJI'S *NO NEW LAND*

KATHLEEN FIRTH
Universitat de Barcelona

When they first arrived in Canada at the beginning of this century, Indians were referred to as Hindus, though most of them were Sikhs, and were called "East Indians" in official records to distinguish them from the indigenous people of the Americas whom Columbus had first misnamed. Later, after the creation of four countries through partitioning and renaming, the somewhat confusing term "South Asians" began to be applied to Canadian immigrants from Pakistan, India, Bangladesh and Sri Lanka. Thus if Columbus was responsible for the original verbal ambiguity because he did not know where he was, Canada has added to the difficulties by pushing a common identity on people who are not all the same.

It was after the liberalization of Canadian immigration laws in the 1960s that these "South Asians" began arriving from parts of the subcontinent other than the Punjab, the homeland of the pioneering Sikhs, and a decade later from Fiji, Africa, the West Indies, Mauritius, Europe and elsewhere[1], meaning that many migrants had taken an indirect route to Canada rather than a direct one from Asia, or had experienced a diaspora that went much farther back in time, as in the case of M.G. Vassanji, whose second novel is the subject of this paper.

Before considering how Vassanji's novel relates to the problems immigrants meet with, it should be remarked that even though Canada, the country in the vanguard of multicultural advance[2], has paradoxically helped to foist on westerners this idea of South Asian homogeneity, it is also in Canada where writers representing diverse areas of the Asiatic diaspora have flourished and on occasion been recognized through prestigious literary awards. Immigrants such as Michael Ondaatje (Sri Lanka), Rohinton Mistry, Suniti Namjoshi, Bharati Mukherjee[3] and Uma Parmeswaran (India), and Himani Bannerji (Bangladesh), who took either a direct or an

indirect route to Canada[4], or others like Neil Bissoondath and Cyril
Dabydeen from the Caribbean, whose diasporic experience, like M. G.
Vassanji's from East Africa, has meant a double transfer in the sense that
these writers are descended from ancestors who were originally taken from
India as indentured workers to supply cheap labour to other parts of the
British Empire[5].

Though South Asian writers established in Canada have moved on
from concern with the politics of ancestral indentureship, their texts, to a
lesser or greater degree, engage with the trials and tribulations of dislocation from their home country and relocation in the Canadian context,
which is another way of coming to terms with the ancient dilemma of
displacement. For be it forced or voluntary, abandoning the place one be-
lieves to be one's home is surely never an easy thing; and in the case of
writers who have undergone a double displacement, the idea of "home" is
perforce a deeply problematic one.

Despite its bleak title, however, *No New Land*[6] engages sympathetically
with the worldviews of several "new" Canadians, most of whom are dou-
bly-alienated souls like Vassanji himself. The novel was written in Toronto,
where he had settled in 1978 and had gone on to establish a literary reputa-
tion ten years' later with the publication of a first novel, entitled *The Gunny
Sack*[7], about which work a few comments might now be made in order to
support a critical response taken on issues raised in the second novel.

Awarded a Regional Commonwealth Prize and hailed as "Africa's answer to *Midnight's Children*"[8], *The Gunny Sack* records the stories of the
descendants through four generations of one Dhanji Govindji, an undis-
tinguished Muslim Indian who abandons the confusions of his Hindu-
Muslim community for the glamour of Zanzibar towards the end of the
nineteenth century. Later, on the East African mainland, Dhanji has a child
to a discarded slave: "The slave trade was over, but the keeping of slaves,
especially women, still persisted on the coast" (11), but he is soon to be
ordered back to his village in India for an arranged marriage that ironically purports to keep him in line and his future offspring racially pure.
Dutiful Dhanji returns to Zanzibar where he has to wait a week for the
next dhow to take him home, a tedious two-month crossing he does not
finally make because fate intervenes in the form of marriage to Fatima,
the daughter of the Zanzibari widow who has provided him with lodg-
ings. Except for one physical flaw – she is "squint-eyed" – , Fatima, we
learn, "would have done proud any Zanzibari harem", for adding to her
many luscious attributes is the fact that she is "extremely fair" (13-14).

This latter description brings up the question of Fatima's progenitor, of whom we are told nothing and about whom we might surmise anything when, years later, Fatima's daughter-in-law wonders about the Zanzibari widow's contribution to the East-African branch of Dhanji Govindji's extended family.

As these comments intend to show, even though it is not essential reading for a proper engagement with Vassanji's second novel, *The Gunny Sack* does address issues of ethnicity and multiculturalism beyond Canada (in contrast, Canada is the setting of all but one of *No New Land*'s eighteen chapters) and it does therefore help to illuminate these concepts for certain Canadians and others like them who assume that the terms have something to do with not being white and of Anglo-Saxon ancestry. What is more, enlarging upon Margaret Atwood's pointed remark about being Canadian in her "Afterword" to *The Journals of Susanna Moodie* where she writes: "we are all immigrants to this place even if we were born here"[9], there is a later statement made by Salman Rushdie, the writer to whom Vassanji has been compared:

> . . . This cultural mixture, this cultural impurity, is certainly of great importance to me as a writer, but I repeat, this is nothing new; I am even coming to suspect that maybe this impurity is the norm in the history of cultures, and that notions of impurity are the aberration – we know the little bit of trouble that was caused in Germany recently by such ideas. Actually, I have been beginning to suspect that there is no such thing as a homogenous culture.[10]

Read in the light of this statement, therefore, the Canadian Multiculturalism Act (also known as Bill C-93), declaring as its goal the preservation and enhancement of Canada's multicultural heritage, seems to be a confirmation of Rushdie's suspicions while it makes of Canada a most forward-looking nation.

The Act has its detractors, nonetheless. Some Canadians see it as an idealistic way of stating the obvious (according to a recent census, 28 per cent of Canadians are descended from more than one ethnic group[11]); others view it as devious rhetoric: declaring that Canada no longer consists officially of only two separate peoples is its way of concealing assimilationist impulses, they say. What is perhaps worse, however, is that for the average Canadian, multiculturalism has nothing to do with ideas and visions, it is merely a word akin to words such as "quaint and folkloric" connoting dressing up and dancing and singing to make a show of 'otherness' for a few happy hours. "It's Disneyland," says writer Neil Bissoondath, "yet that's what multiculturalism means to most people, that's where it's most valuable to the politicians."[12]

Canadian writers like Vassanji of "South Asian" classification, as well as those whose classification likewise reveals that their ancestry does not lead back to fathers and mothers belonging to the two so-called founding nations[13], are also described (i.e. classified) as "ethnic" writers. But as conscientious Canadians have observed, this term, deriving from the Greek root meaning "a nation", is superfluous in the etymological sense since all Canadians, including the English and French, are "ethnic"[14]. Through usage it has nevertheless acquired the meaning of "foreign", so that writers labelled in this way are not understood as forming part of the mainstream but rather as representatives of this or that group who are usually expected to write about certain themes in a certain way.

It goes without saying that the notions of ethnicity and multiculturalism are extremely complex ones, too complex for any government to eradicate through legislation. It perhaps remains the role of the talented Canadian writers who *happen* to belong to ethnic minorities to show through their creative enterprise that the ideal behind such legislation is in the end a worthy ideal.

⋆   ⋆   ⋆   ⋆

The fact that Vassanji's second novel appeared soon after the promulgation of Bill C-93 when funds became available to publish writings by ethnic minorities does not imply that the writer had jumped aboard the cultural bandwagon. Even a cursory reading of *No New Land*, or a reading that is not influenced by the success of his first novel, reveals Vassanji as a very serious writer because he writes convincingly about his community with its "warts and all", as Salman Rushdie would say[15]. If Canada represents no new land for the Lalanis and other immigrants it is not because Vassanji focuses on the hopelessness of their condition, but because he has chosen to write about the sort of things that concern human beings everywhere, like love and death and money and friendship and family loyalties, and these are things that have little to do with a writer's ethnicity. On the other hand, the Canadian context of the novel, often a disturbing and humiliating context, is never ignored; indeed, most things occur in the shadow of the CN Tower, that sleek icon of technology and progress that holds mesmeric fascination for the hapless protagonist.

Having arrived in Toronto with his wife and two children following the nationalizations of Asian property in Tanzania, shoe-salesman Nurdin Lalani sets about finding himself a job commensurable with the one he had in Dar, one befitting his status as man of the house and son of a respected Asian elder and prominent businessman back home before the Africanizations. Confidence begins to verge on despair when he is repeatedly turned down because of his accent, though the ostensible explanation is that he lacks "Canadian experience". Against this he has no answer; but to salvage what remains of his sinking self-esteem Nurdin resolves to "try different accents, practise idioms, buy shoes to raise [his] height. Deodorize [himself] silly" (44). His efforts are wasted. In the next interview, attempting to impress the polite white manager at Eatons with his experience in sales and his command of English, he gets carried away and says the wrong things, with the result that he is not given the job on the grounds that he is "... perhaps ... overqualified" (48).

Ironies abound subtly and intelligently in this work. The menfolk of Sixty-nine Rosecliffe Park, the high-rise block housing the Lalanis and well over two hundred other immigrant families, are frequently unemployed for many months but they draw comfort from the meetings for chitchat and tea downstairs in the lobby, in emulation of a famous teashop back in Dar. There they discuss life and religion and community politics, for the Dar immigrants, we are told, "love to debate" (49). The lobby clique is also a source of information on employment and immigration:

> ... Nurdin was told there how he could get a job as a subway-car cleaner at night, working with some of the other fellows of Sixty-nine. The job was easy. You just did a few cars and then found an isolated one where you played cards for the remainder of the night. How do you get such a job? You simply had to "oil the hands" of the supervisor. "What-what?" he said, incredulous. "Here? In Canada?" "Tell him, Uncle," someone said. And they all turned to look at the man they called Uncle, a stout, elderly former businessman, who spoke the wisdom of experience. "Yes. Just give your first week's salary." (88)

Meanwhile, the wives and mothers are out working at menial jobs, or upstairs running little local industries on the side, like Gulshan Bai's takeaway tiffin, or Sheru Mama's chappatis "at four for a dollar, cheaper wholesale" and a babysitting service provided at the same time (61). A lively exception to the idlers in the lobby is Ram Deen, an Asian fellow from the Caribbean who sells holy meat to those who identify themselves as belonging to "the brotherhood" before the I LOVE ALLAH sign he has painted on his apartment door (62). But mostly, the unemployed males of block Sixty-nine display industry only for a frantic half hour in the late afternoon, dashing around to "clean up at home, sweeping away any sign of degeneracy, giving the television time enough to cool" (66) before the bread-winning wife and the children get home.

Despite the surface humour, Vassanji's purpose here and elsewhere in this work is to draw the reader's attention to one of the saddest aspects of the immigrants' lot, which is the ghettoization that occurs when people arrive in Canada and find themselves living in their closed ethnic communities and rarely engaging with the larger society. But if Vassanji has no solutions, he at least offers the issue for thought and debate, in emulation perhaps of his characters in the lobby at Sixty-nine. For as "new Canadian" writer Rohinton Mistry has pointed out: on the one hand, there is the larger society demanding "Canadian experience", which makes little sense to new arrivals, on the other, until the realization dawns that it is a polite way of saying that there are no jobs for them. "Canadian experience" thus acquires mysterious connotations: there has to be something very special about it if one has done the same kind of work elsewhere, but which work is not the same thing, according to the prospective employers. (Nurdin's failure to find employment as a shoe salesman, for example). When one eventually finds a job, it is at the lowest possible salary grade, the other employees are mostly immigrants and predominantly females (such as Nurdin's cleaning job in a donut store downtown where all the waitresses are East Europeans). Occasionally, a white male appears in the ranks, but he soon disappears. And where has he gone? Higher up the ladder where the workforce becomes increasingly white and predominantly male (like the manager at Eatons who interviews Nurdin)[16].

If Vassanji is ironically suggesting along with Mistry that "ghettoization" and "Canadian experience" are in fact synonymous terms, he does not leave matters there. His moral responsibility is towards his readership and his own community, and he would be serving neither well were he to subscribe to what Edward Said has described elsewhere as the politics of blame. For while we are made to empathize with a predicament that generates in Nurdin a process of emasculation and self contempt, he is also portrayed as an essentially functionless male, a decent human being but one who simply allows things to happen to him, rarely instigating action or ideas himself. What is more, he suffers from the double vision common to all immigrants: that looking forward and yearning backward which is symbolized and heightened in Nurdin's case by his father's photograph on the wall next to the window through which he contemplates the CN Tower. As the rot sets in, he takes to sitting alone in the darkened room, avoiding the "hard eyes" that glare at him in "relentless judgement" from the photograph, while he attempts to address the lofty structure in the distance that is "blinking its signals into the hazy darkness" (82-83).

With a regular job at the Ontario Addiction Centre obtained through the help of Romesh, a West Indian of Indian origins who enters his life out of the blue, Nurdin steps into the world "out there" (80), but it is a world full of pitfalls and greater confusions. For while it is true that in the mosque, the place where one's "real worth is measured" (89), he can now proudly announce that he has secured a regular job downtown and need not disclose the menial nature of his tasks ("Say manager," his wife suggests, "You do manage supply rooms" (126), it is also true that the religious strictures and observances of the old world are either impracticable or making impossible demands on one's proper conduct whenever one finds oneself "out there":

> Braless women with lively breasts under blouses and T-shirts that simply sucked your eyeballs out. Buttocks breaking out of shorts. And when you saw these twin delights nuzzling a bicycle seat, doing a gentle rhythmic dance of their own in the dazzling heat and among the trees and flowers and the smells of nature in the park – why, you had to be sure you were dressed right (141).

To make matters worse, there is the irrepressible Romesh, who has severed the links with his Hindu past, taking over the task of regulating Nurdin's life as Nurdin's father had done in Africa. After introducing him to the forbidden tastes of pork and beer, Romesh makes light of Nurdin's "bouts of guilt" (141), and, sensing that Nurdin's true problem is lust – "That big wife of yours not letting you have it?" (139) – , provides simple solutions like taking him to a peepshow on the way home, or, when that tactic fails, encouraging his involvement with an attractive Indian widow they meet through their jobs at the Addiction Centre. Nurdin never partakes of the forbidden pleasures of the flesh with the willing widow, but as one of the free thinkers of his community had pointed out to him earlier on, after Nurdin's original act of incontinence: "You are *already* changed when you think about eating pork" (136).

It is through interaction with the immigrants whose lives interweave with his own that Nurdin approaches a modicum of understanding of his place in the new land. But his dilemma is never completely resolved. He no longer shares the nostalgia of a wife who is "married to God" (138) and whose life becomes meaningful only when her spiritual leader in East Africa finally agrees to go and settle in Canada, for she expects him to sanction her idea that one should not strive to become assimilated to the godless Canadians. Worse, Nurdin despairs of ever winning back the loyalties of his teenage daughter, who is gradually becoming absorbed by Canadian ways and has begun to reveal shame and contempt for the ways of her parents. And these sad truths engender more confusions as Nurdin gropes his way towards the self-knowledge that his Canadian experience is forcing upon him: that his father, long dead but still exerting tyrannical pressure, is the overriding cause of his personal dilemma. Nor can he find solace in the utilitarian logic displayed by the community leader who insists: "to become westernized... is what we've opted for by coming here" (72) when this character abandons his community for the glamour of life at the top.

These, then, are some of the issues raised by Vassanji's second novel. As I observed above, he does not attempt to offer solutions, but by portraying a number of complex human beings whose common bond, largely because they are classified as "new" Canadians, is their sense of otherness, he is providing stories that are serving to enrich the host country and at the same time helping to forge the way to a hopeful new land where classifying people and adhering to notions of cultural purity will be things of the past.

NOTES

1. For further details see: Hugh Johnston, *The East Indians in Canada*, Ottawa: Canada's Ethnic Groups Series, Booklet No.5, published by the Canadian Historical Association with the support of the Multicultural Program, Government of Canada, 1984.
2. Bill C-93, the "Act for the preservation and enhancement of multiculturalism in Canada", was passed on July 21st, 1988.
3. Purporting to find Canada a hypocritical society in its treatment of immigrants, Bharati Mukherjee left after a highly productive writing period to settle in the United States.
4. Ondaatje, for example, took an "indirect route", leaving his native Ceylon (today's Sri Lanka) for England in 1954 when he was eleven, later leaving England for Canada in 1962.

5. Exploited largely on the Caribbean sugar plantations or on the railway constructions in Africa, the indentured workers, or "coolies" as they were called, were as essential to the British Imperial design as were the African slaves they replaced after emancipation during the second half of the 19th century; indeed, albeit unwittingly and unwillingly, the slaves and coolies were the real empire builders.

6. M.G. Vassanji, *No New Land*, Toronto: McClelland & Stewart,1991. All further references will be to this edition and placed in brackets after quotes in the text.

7. M.G. Vassanji, *The Gunny Sack*, London: Heinemann African Writers Series, 1989. All further references will be to this edition and placed in brackets after quotes in the text.

8. Blurb taken from the *Toronto Star*. Displayed on covers of the editions cited at notes 6 & 7 above.

9. Margaret Atwood, "Afterword" to *The Journals of Susanna Moodie*, Toronto: Oxford University Press, 1970.

10. Salman Rushdie, "Minority Literatures in a Multi-Cultural Society" in eds. Kirsten Holt Petersen and Anna Rutherford, *Displaced Persons*, Mundelstrup: Dangaroo Press, 1988, p.35.

11. "Introduction", to eds. Linda Hutcheon & Marion Richmond, *Other Solitudes: Canadian Multicultural Fictions*, Toronto: Oxford University Press, 1990, p.12.

12. Neil Bissondath interviewed by Aruna Srivastava in ibid, p.317.

13. Though a further misnomer, "founding nations" is used to refer to the Canadians descended from the first European settlers from France and Britain, in total disregard for the Native peoples of Canada.

14. See Linda Hutcheon in "Introduction", op. cit., p.2; or Janice Kulyk Keefer (pp.39-40) and the views of other writers classified as "ethnics" in Jeanne Delabaere, ed., *Multiple Voices: Recent Canadian Fiction*, Mundelstrup, Dangaroo Press, 1990, passim.

15. Salman Rushdie, *op. cit.*, p.40.

16. Rohinton Mistry interviewed by Dagmar Novak in eds. Linda Hutcheon & Marion Richmond, *op. cit.*, p.256.

REMEMBERING INDIA: HOMELAND, HERITAGE OR HINDRANCE IN THE WRITING BY WOMEN OF THE INDIAN DIASPORA IN BRITAIN

RANJANA SIDHANTA ASH

The paper, a brief argument without any clear resolution, examines the nature of the Indian connection in selected works written by women of Indian origin in Britain. The geo-political phrase, "of Indian origin", has been interpreted strictly to define writers who were born to Indian parents in India or Britain and are now domiciled in Britain. It is possibly a pedantic exactness as the official British category of "Asian" includes those from the four countries of the Subcontinent within the Commonwealth: India, Pakistan, Bangladesh and Sri Lanka. However, on the occasion of the 50th anniversary of India's independence the paper's focus is restricted to the perceptions and visions of India in the fiction and poetry of selected women writers with an Indian connection.

During the celebrations which took place among Indian Immigrant communities dotted in various urban centres of Britain to mark the 50th year of independence of India from British rule, there has been a flurry of enthusiasm for some vision of the "motherland", for its national liberation struggle and for its cultural heritage of music, dance, poetry, presented by distinguished artists and performers invited from India. Yet, over the five decades of postwar Indian immigration to Britain, the Indian connection has been problematic, subject to the frustrations and challenges in the lives of immigrants, in the inter-generational shifts, in identifying with India as the homeland, and cultural changes affecting the life-styles and value judgements of immigrants. An exploration of the representations of India, as remembered and imaginatively created by women from different generations of the Indian diaspora in Britain today, is studied from the perspective of its significance to the Indian diaspora in general and to the host community, or that element within it which shows any interest in such writing.

Formulated in simplistic terms and avoiding the actual complexities of cultural interaction between the Indian minorities and their British hosts whether they be neighbours, workmates, fellow students, the paper considers the impact of the Indian nexus, albeit through literature, on the diaspora's cultural development. Articulated as queries they are as follows:

Does the India that is received through the stories and poems, the plays and films by writers who are themselves part of the diaspora reinforce an Indian identity embedded in the notion of India as homeland or motherland?

Does such literary inscription contribute to different kinds of cultural interaction such as biculturalism – possessing two separate cultures – or cultural hybridity? The latter is described variously as occupying a space in between the two cultures confronted by the immigrant – her natal or parental inheritance and the new British experience – or producing an entirely new fused or synthesised culture.[1]

Since this is writing by women, how far does the diasporic view of changing women's lives and feminism colour the memories or perceptions of India and relate them to the changes affecting gender roles in Britain and in India where feminist consciousness follows its own social activism?

Finally, as the process of adjustment continues and a second generation grows into maturity and there is now a third generation within the Indian minority, does the Indian connection retain its relevance for an Indian immigrant who, by now, is a British citizen by naturalisation or birth? In a Britain where non-white immigrants have had to bear the many manifestations of racism there is evidence of cultural marginalisation through the loss of language and knowledge of ethnic pasts on the one hand, and an indifferent and dismissive attitude towards minority languages and cultures by British institutions on the other. At such a juncture the young Asian can either retreat into a regressive nativism or accept the stronger pull of adjustment and change. Whether the first signs of the adoption of modified names, of changing attire and ways of life indicate the inevitability of assimilation, as in the USA, is difficult to predict. In such a transitional period the Indian link may prove to be a liability, a hindrance to being accepted as a true Brit, or it may provide the security of a perennial heritage that cannot be exterminated.

The memory of immigrants tends to fluctuate and invent, or recall with great accuracy, depending on the nature and degree of separation from the homeland. Since the bulk of Indian immigration to Britain from the late 1940s and early 1950s to the 1970s, after which it became a mere trickle, was voluntary, to improve economic and educational prospects, the conventional use of "diaspora" to describe this immigration is not correct. The real connotation of "diaspora" originated in the context of the enforced dispersal of Jews in ancient times, of Africans taken into slavery and indentured Indian labourers forced to migrate to different parts of the British Empire. With the Indian male immigrants in Britain there was no initial sense of losing one's home, of going into exile, because there was the idea of returning to the homeland having earned a sizeable income. But for Indian women who were brought as the dependants of male relations, as wives and daughters, there was little free choice. The dislocation and anxiety of being marooned in a strange land, without knowing English and afraid of racist abuse, even violence, affected Asian women cooped up in their cold dank rooms in some immigrant area of British inner cities, as expressed in their oral and written testimonies (See Wilson 1978; Chatterjee & Islam 1990 & 1993).

There were other circumstances to make one an exile, as experienced by Attia Hosain, the doyenne of Indian women writers in Britain. Born into a prominent upper-class North Indian Muslim family, she saw her world disintegrate with the advent of Partition and the creation of the Muslim republic of Pakistan. As her family became divided, with some migrating to Pakistan and others remaining in India, she came to London with her diplomat husband in 1947. For her, the stay in Britain, which has continued, has been experienced as exile, though she was an intimate of the postwar London world of letters and knew important writers and critics. The India that she created was essentially an India that existed before Partition and was to disintegrate and even disappear in its aftermath.

> The reality of exile was harsh. Protective layers of privilege, of family name and relationships nurtured through generations, were stripping away. I was a stranger living amongst strangers, and idealism was not enough. Stories crowded my thoughts, linking me with a lost, secure world. Once again, as a refuge in the mind, I began to write... (1988c).

These sentiments, expressed by her in a newspaper article several years after the publication of her sole collection of short stories, *Phoenix Fled,* and her only novel, *Sunlight on a Broken Column*, give an insight into the motivation of her writing. However, as a consummate stylist and a master of her craft she was able to capture, without sentimentality or excessive nostalgic memories, the composite culture of North India, that blend of Persian and Indian, of Muslim and Hindu, of Urdu and Hindi and the new element of anglicisation which generated culture clash and divided loyalties within families. Her concern with reality and her choice of characters across the highly stratified semi-feudal society of the day reveal an Indian canvas painted with a more complex interpretation of social realism than was then emerging as a major Indian literary movement through the writings of the Progressive Writers Association formed in 1936 (Coppola, 1974). Hosain's India did not shy away from poverty and exploitation, but she was able to craft stories in which the social and economic truth of servants and retainers in feudal households, of women abandoned by husbands, of villagers left destitute was expressed through imagery, and emotion controlled by elegant diction, wit and honesty. An old village woman, a family retainer, is left alone in her hut which is burnt by soldiers hunting for marauders during the savage riots that accompanied Partition. A middle-class young wife, out of purdah, is scandalised by the antics of her husband and guests at her first cocktail party ("The First Party", 1988a). This particular story, included in a much used anthology (Holmstrom, 1990), evokes the interest, as readers, of British-Asian girls who identify with the character's predicament of attempting to adapt to changing ways and being repelled by many elements of western mores, an ambivalence that is widespread in the Asian diaspora.

Sunlight on a Broken Column, Hosain's only novel, is an outstanding fictional account of the life of a North Indian upper-class Muslim woman exposed to the many changes of modernisation and orthodoxy in prewar India until the bitter shattering of an entire way of life during Partition when her family is hopelessly divided and the very house in which she was born and grew up is confiscated. It is a kind of female bildungsroman that charts the journey of a young woman, bilingual and bicultural like others of her class, enjoying English literature at school and Urdu-Persian classics at home. She overcomes her cocooned privileged existence and family conservatism to fashion her own life, choose her husband, and find the strength to withstand the tragedy of his death and her personal and cultural loss in post-Partition India. The novel, used for A level and undergraduate work in Britain, has proved to be enormously popular with a second and third generation of Asian girls, especially those from Muslim homes who identify with Laila, the novel's narrator and protagonist.

The presentation of India in the ten novels by Kamala Markandaya, who has lived in Britain for decades, reflects what she considers to be a very personalised view of an Indian, not meant to be typical or representative. "...I think of myself as an Indian writer ...In everything I say I speak for myself. I am not, and never have been, a spokeswoman or spokesperson, if you prefer, for India..." (Markandaya, 1976:27). It is an India that crosses the author's own privileged class and caste position at the top of South Indian society, into villages and city slums, creating a wide range of characters from minor royalty down to the lowliest of landless labourers. One wonders whether the predominance of the Indian context in her fiction stems from her very clearly articulated stance as an expatriate writer. Markandaya does not see herself as an immigrant. "This term, to my mind, (a little like exile) suggests someone who leaves her country under pressure – persecution or ideological/political dissent: not so in my case..."[2].

Expatriation, more than exile, which tends to be overwhelming in its waves of nostalgia, produces a bifocality which enables the writer to perceive both the homeland and the new land, their respective distances shifting according to her subjectivity and external circumstances. Regular visits to India, alternating with residence in London, should, on one level, be an ideal situation for writing that can maintain a certain balance and objectivity in the representation of both locations. Kamala Markandaya's fiction is heavily centred on an India in which Indians interact with British characters who, in novels which are set in pre-independence times, tend to be administrators, or, when the setting is post-1947, technical experts. She suggests romantic attachments across racial divides as in *Some Inner Fury* and *The Coffer Dams*, in which the attachments do not find fulfilment (1955 & 1969). Hers is an essentially romanticised view of India despite themes of rural poverty and urban misery, despite a critical approach to contemporary issues such as the depredation of the land for the sake of tourist hotels or the confiscation of tribal forest homes to build dams (1982 &1969).

Markandaya's India diverges far from her own upper-class position. The novel which won her international acclaim, her very first, *Nectar in a Sieve*, set in train the kind of characters with whom she appeared to empathise – rural labouring women – helping their husbands through poverty and hard times to keep the family intact; mothers from urban artisan homes, determined to protect daughters seduced by film producers; women refusing to succumb to adversity (1982 & 1973). Heroic and admirable though these women were, they lacked credibility partly because of the melodramatic narrative lines and partly because of Markandaya's elegant style. Her sentences with their oblique allusions and subtle undertones, reminiscent at times of Henry James, sit incongruously in the dust and grime of her locations. It remains open to debate whether Markandaya's huge popularity with her Anglo-American readers – *Nectar in a Sieve* is one of the first bestsellers by an Indian writing in English and has always been in print since its publication in 1954 – depends on presenting rural poverty as bearable. The narrator heroine, Rukmani, a strong woman who withstands all adversity, comments on the plight of poor peasants with calm dispassion:

> To those who live by the land there must always come times of hard-ship, of fear and of hunger, even as there are years of plenty. This is one of the truths of our existence as those who live by the land know: that sometimes we eat and sometimes we starve... (1982:136).

Markandaya's India does not seem to evoke much interest in the Asian diaspora, perhaps because so many have come from rural backgrounds and may not entirely accept Rukmani's attitude. The book which does resonate with her diasporic readers is *The Nowhere Man*, a profoundly moving novel of an older Indian immigrant in a London suburb (1973). Srinivas has lived through the horrors of the blitz along with his British neighbours; a son served in the War and is well assimilated. Srinivas, who has never been able to accept Britain as the colonial oppressor like his more politicised friend, finds himself the target of racist thugs in one of the waves of racism of the 1950s and 1960s. He must now face the truth. He, away from his own land for decades, has nowhere to go, "a nowhere man look-ing for a nowhere city" (1973:174). It is the classic isolation of the immi-grant who must live on the margins no matter how he constructs his own subjectivity about his new land. Srinivas has been prepared to overlook British imperialism's record; he has maintained neighbourly relations with his suburban acquaintances; he even has a British woman staying with him now that he is a widower. Yet he remains the outsider, the target for racist violence and abuse at one extreme and little more than an ac-knowledgement of his presence by others.

The expatriate vision of India of an Indian woman who belongs to the second generation of the Asian diaspora in Britain has to be disentangled from her seamless narratives in which past and present, India, or rather, Calcutta, Britain and the USA are enmeshed. Sunetra Gupta (b. 1965), from West Bengal, has lived in Britain since coming over to do postgraduate research at London's Imperial College of Science from Princeton University in the United States and is now a fellow of Merton College, Ox-ford. A biological scientist by profession, she has written three novels which are as unusual in structure as in their style (1992, 1993 & 1995). Calcutta, America and Britain, with occasional forays to Europe, get interwoven as

Gupta's characters move between past memories, present fantasies and future dreams. The Indian connection is strongest in her first novel, *Memories of Rain,* a passionate love story which ends unhappily for the Bengali woman, Moni, when she can no longer live with her English husband's infidelity. Moni's memories and associations, which Gupta elaborates through an extended stream of consciousness technique, revive her life in Calcutta, the sexual passion she and Anthony experienced as the Calcutta monsoons unleashed their fury. Moni relives past happiness as family and friends are remembered along with a great deal of Bengali literary culture. Sunetra Gupta has the advantage over several of her fellow diasporic writers in being fully bilingual in Bengali and English and able to do her own translations of lines of poetry by Tagore and Jibanananda, of snatches of Tagore songs, used to heighten Moni's grief as well as providing consolation. Calcutta finally is raised from its figurative role providing suitable tropes for the various stages of love in Moni's life to that of the motherland, providing refuge to her as she returns to her parents and native city from the cold and treacherous English husband, with her little daughter. *Memories of Rain* provides an India that is both a cultural reality and a metaphor, the symbolic shelter provided by the mother and her home.

The representations of India, literally and figuratively, in Gupta's two other novels, *The Glassblower's Breath* and *Moonlight Into Marzipan,* are more difficult to analyse because of the convoluted lines of narrative and a deliberate lack of temporal and spatial framing which prevents individual images and tropes from being isolated. On one level, both novels reveal comments, descriptions and fictional detail that illustrate Gupta's own liberal, even left-wing stance, on such issues as the rise of Hindu fundamentalism, or the destruction of the old culture of Calcutta as a new class of entrepreneurs buys up old property and destroys it to rebuild a Calcutta of high-rise luxury apartments (1993:226-33). However, neither these wider social perspectives, nor the fact that they are being displaced outside their native city, is more than marginal in the way Gupta develops the inner lives of the Indians who are her main characters.

One occasionally gets an interesting discussion on the complexity of changing one's identity, of trying to recapture lost ethnicity and language in *Moonlight into Marzipan.* Yuri Sen, an ambiguous character that some have seen as a Satanic incarnation, though Bengali by birth, has been educated in England. When he suddenly gives up a place at Cambridge and returns to India because he wants to be a Bengali, his father taunts him: "You think you can become a Bengali just like that... just by immersing yourself in the culture after so many years?" The mother reassures the son by proclaiming his Bengali blood and that he is literate in Bengali. The son knows better because he cannot really comprehend Tagore and has lost out on living as a Bengali (1995:116-7).

Moonlight Into Marzipan can be read as an allegory – the futility of trying to solve major socio-economic problems such as poverty through individual gestures. When an idealistic young scientist turns his wife's copper ear-stud into grass and is invited to work in England, he nurtures hopes of helping to solve the problem of Third World hunger. His wife says earnestly when told by Yuri that she should try not to make Britain her home:

> We shall most definitely return after five years ...We come not in search of creature comforts, as many have done before us, we come not in search of a better life but only to fulfil a mission which, when it is complete, will release us to return (ibid. 51).

Unfortunately, the experiment does not succeed. The wife commits suicide on discovering her husband's relationship with a European woman. One can read many allegorical interpretations into the failure – one more example of an indigenous attempt to overcome food scarcity being frustrated by western interference or, on a more moral plane, the seduction of the East by the blandishments of the West.

The significance of being bilingual, seen in Sunetra Gupta's use of Bengali literary culture, is reinforced in the writings by two women whose knowledge of two languages creates an India enriched by both the tongues they use. Ketaki Kushari Dyson writes in both her native Bengali and English while Sujata Bhatt experiments with Gujarati, her mother tongue, within her mainly English poetry.

Ketaki Kushari Dyson divides her works between her native Bengali and English which, as an Oxford-based scholar, she uses for her scholarly works and some of her verse. Unlike Sujata Bhatt, who introduces Gujarati within a poem written in English, Dyson separates her two languages but, interestingly, crosses cultural boundaries in both. A novel, in Bengali, and a recent play set in an Oxford suburb engage with Indian and English characters whose cultural milieu, though disparate, reflect the increasing commonality of intellectuals grappling with their own alienation from global consumerist values. Dyson's India is that of the cultivated Bengali, steeped in Tagore and contemporary urbanised Calcutta life, which, far from weighing on the younger generation, excites them (1980). Her biculturality, rather than hybridity, can be found in her English verse where she shifts from Indian, or more accurately, Bengali images of terracotta temples, temple dancers, flooded rice fields to Oxford and English gardens (1983). Dyson has probably contributed more to a knowledge of Tagore through her excellent translations of some of his poetry and through her scholarly research on Victoria Ocampo's friendship with Tagore, an intriguing relationship between an Indian cultural icon and an Argentinian feminist. The Indian perspective of a bilingual woman writer can be seen in Dyson's essay on the subject, "Forging a Bilingual Identity: a Writer's Testimony" (1994), a record of frustration in a British literary milieu, heavily anglocentric and prejudiced against translated texts.

For Sujata Bhatt, her mother tongue has been a lifeline for her poet's voice. The loss of language, possibly the most serious deprivation faced by the second and third generation of Asian immigrants, has been central to much of her verse. The strongest image in her well known poem, "Search for my Tongue", is that of the little girl at a railway station selling water to the passengers. Here, Bhatt interweaves Gujarati and English to depict the girl's cry because "I can't think of her in English", as she admits (1988). It underlines a fundamental issue in the representation of India in diasporic writing that is mainly in English, since India's people, except for the small minority, no more than two per cent of the population, use their own regional languages and not English. To have to depict their lives, their perceptions and feelings in English creates problems which Bhatt says cannot be solved through English.

India in Bhatt's poetry is visualised through its women. Bhatt ranges through childhood memories of grandmothers and great-aunts, of mothers and daughters. There are women imprisoned by tradition like the young widow who "thinks she should have burned on her husband's funeral pyre" ("Buffaloes" 1988); of nine year old Sharda, trapped by flames in the prayer room; of Jyoti, who slaps henna paste on her palms because she likes red though the hands are "blistered, scratched..." (1991). Bhatt's espousal of her mother tongue resonates with second generation Asians who recognise their loss of not knowing their parental languages (Ash, 1995).

The Indian connection assumes a more problematic aspect in the writings of a younger generation of women, each of whom has published at least one novel in Britain and whose short fiction appears in British magazines. Their positions are not necessarily similar though they focus on their dual selves – part British and Indian – in their fiction. For Leena Dhingra the connection was unsettling perhaps because she came to Britain while a little girl with her parents who had lost their homes in that part of the Punjab which became Pakistan. The sense of being "homeless" that consumed Partition refugees, despite later security – Dhingra's father was in UNESCO –, probably affected her from childhood, and an education which was divided between India and Europe contributed to an early confusion of her cultural identity. Her much anthologised piece, "Breaking Out Of The Labels", begins with her quandary:

> I first came to this country nearly thirty years ago during which time I have fallen into, fitted and resisted a series of multifarious labels from: a girl from India, an Indian girl, a coloured, a Paki, a black, a wog, an Asian, and recently graduated to becoming a member of an ethnic minority (1987:103).

Her novel *Amritvela* revolves round a journey to visit her aunts in Delhi by an Indian woman living in Britain whose marriage seems to be failing. Shahrukh Husain analyses the work as the diasporic Asian's "journey to the promised land" (1990). In Britain, Meera, the book's protagonist, feels herself to be a misfit. The visit to her Indian family is a kind of therapy and she returns "re-connected". On the way out to India, sitting in the aeroplane, in Meera's words, "I feel myself to be suspended between two cultures... the halfway point between East and West..." (1988:1). After her happy time with aunts and great-aunts and their elderly friends, and their loving care with what she will eat and wear, Meera feels a "subtle transformation" in herself.

> Throughout my stay I have searched – for questions, for answers, for clues that would show me the way... Now, paradoxically, I am leaving and feeling I've arrived, and my questions have dissolved, leaving me unburdened and light, almost as though I'd found whatever it was... (ibid. 168).

The near-spiritual nuances of a journey to India found by Meera, akin to those sought by so many Westerners who seek solace and enlightenment from Indian holy men and women, have been put aside by Dhingra who is now working on a book on nationalist India, a special militant nationalism that combined late 19th century revolutionary ideology with a revivalist notion of India's golden age that had been desecrated by India's conquerors. Her documentary drama based on the life of her great-uncle, the Indian patriot, Madan Lal Dhingra, who was hanged in Pentonville prison in London in 1909 for killing Curzon Willie, a British colonial administrator, may appear to be a major shift from Dhingra's fiction. In her novel and short stories she has viewed India in a personalised context – within a family or an individualised perception of the Indian self and the other. Now, it is a focus on an India conceptualised as a political entity around which real characters discourse on conflicting methods of achieving national liberation, on India's cultural decline and the possibility of spiritual regeneration. Yet, because of the central figure's connection with Dhingra's family, Indian nationalism is treated on two levels: on the macro-philosophical and its significance for individual Indians; and on how being colonised and desiring freedom affect the individual psyche.

The Asian Women Writers' Workshop, founded in London in 1984 by a group of Asian women from India and Pakistan, included Ravinder Randhawa, Meera Syal, Rahila Gupta and Dhingra. It encouraged Asian women to write and get their work discussed and evaluated within a collective of like-minded people. Its problematic relationship with the Indian Subcontinent from which they or their parents originated can be judged from the introduction to its first anthology of prose and poetry, entitled *Right of Way*. In the introduction there is no reference to India other than to its regional languages and literatures:

> Though we see ourselves as British-based Asian women, not all of us were born and bred here, and we brought with us different cultural and literary influences. This affected our critical responses. Some of us found it difficult to appreciate translations of Urdu or Bengali poetry... Criticisms of work seemed to be much easier on political grounds. Positions were clearly drawn and we were able to say about the content, for example, this is classist, patronising, communalist, heterosexist, or whatever (1988:2-3).

The homeland is becoming the "otherland", known merely through the parental connection and whatever ethnic links have been established by the family. British education, which was the main conduit of their intellectual development, has cut them off from the nourishing streams that nurture biculturalism. It did not teach them their familial languages – the mother or father tongue; it did not include Indian history or geography in the school curriculum except as the occasional module or project. British media does not find countries of the former Empire newsworthy unless they are engulfed by disaster. The Indian connection is reduced to the family circle and "community" links. The periodic visits to the "motherland" become visits to "grandparent" land. Bilingualism has declined, reducing the Indian language to an orality solely used within the family.

Such linguistic loss, as acknowledged, is accompanied by the loss of the entire fabric of Indian literary cultures, unless available in translation, which is not always appreciated aesthetically.

Yet the sense of being Indian remains, though with mixed emotions as the consciousness of becoming a split personality develops. They are Punjabi, Gujerati, Hindu, Muslim, high caste, low caste or whatever Indian ethnicity is projected in the family and community, but outside they are "Asians", or "coloured", or described more pejoratively. Theirs is now a hyphenated identity which receives the British establishment's acceptance – British-Asian and its derivatives such as British-Muslim, British-Bengali.

But the growth of racism and the older generation's apprehension of their children, especially their daughters, being tempted by the permissiveness they perceive in British society, are contributing to a siege mentality on the part of some Asian minority communities and a desire to maintain and uphold their version of ethnic particularity. Ignorance and fear, hyphenated identities without a comprehensive knowledge or experience of being Indian other than belonging to a specific part of that big country provoke some voices within Indian and Pakistani communities to invent ways of eating, dressing, and, above all, of gender roles that are believed to be in conformity with their specific ethnic identity. India's cultural plurality gets dismissed as in the misconception that all Hindus are vegetarians or all Muslim women should be veiled. A narrow regionalism and sectarianism overtake the Indian ideal of "Unity Through Diversity" and the younger British-Punjabis, British-Gujeratis and other hyphenated members of the Indian diaspora in Britain find it difficult to perceive an India that is beyond their own cultural markers. This has become particularly noticeable with the rise of religious fundamentalism – Sikh, Muslim, Hindu – and the difficulty of accepting an India of many faiths, many races and ways of life. The notion that to be Indian signifies adherence to Hinduism and that Muslims must be from Pakistan are among the misconceptions being assiduously promoted by religious fundamentalists among Asian communities in Britain (Sahgal 1992).

Two writers associated with the Asian Women Writers in the early years, Ravinder Randhawa and Meera Syal, depict essentially Punjabi families from India in their novels. Randhawa's first novel, *A Wicked Old Woman*, is a complex narrative involving several characters, mainly Punjabi, over three generations. Randhawa's many themes may be essentialised as the difficulty and psychological confusion that face women from Asian families who want different goals and lifestyles from those desired by their parents. The conflict is never clearly defined nor are generational attitudes always predictable. Kulwant, the wayward heroine of Indian Punjabi origin but brought up in Britain, the product of British state schools, Labour politics, and urban culture involving media publicity, drugs and racism, sees her parents as the bearers of Indian culture with some ambivalence:

> exotic bric-brac from a country that for some was home, for others nothing more than a distant childhood memory, and for those born here a patchwork land transmitted through parents' stories of places, people, happenings: an infrastructure kept alive with letters, imbibed with baby milk, mixed with rotis and savoured with the mature taste of chillies. Throwing up some who strived to be more Indian than the Indians over there, though born in England as they were. Was it a testimony to the power of transference from generation to generation, or a testimony to the force of the hostile world outside (1987:31).

Randhawa is not precise about the Indian values she ascribes to Kulwant's parents beyond strict rules of decorum and modesty for their daughters, behaviour which excludes British boyfriends and any thought of crossing race, class and caste barriers in marriage. In an imaginary dialogue Kulwant has with her mother she assigns notions of *dharma* in the mother's concern for the right path according to one's place in society, something that Kulwant has forgotten or not been able to find in her dislocated world. India is the repository of moral certainty; Britain induces confusion and moral relativism (ibid. 54).

For Syal's heroine, pre-pubescent Meena, growing up on the outskirts of a West Midlands conurbation, there is an initial rejection of her Punjabi Indian identity through her obsession with Anita, a working-class English school mate who lives in the same village. *Anita and Me,* Syal's first novel after a string of successful radio, television and film scripts, might be described as the formulaic diaspora novel. It is a journey of discovery by a second generation immigrant who must find herself through her cultural roots and the promising future which the new land will provide now that she can integrate past and present selves, place India and Britain, family and neighbours in their rightful slots.

India, initially, appears as a troublesome and even frightening place as the little girl listens to her mother's stories of life in a Punjab village during Partition. Syal paints these memories with a judicious mixture of the exotic, the banal and the fearful:

But gradually I got bored, and then jealous of this past that excluded me; she had milked goats, stroked peacocks, pulled sugar cane from the earth as a mid-morning snack. She had even seen someone stabbed to death, much later on when the family had moved to Delhi and partition riots stalked the streets like a ravenous animal (1996:36).

India is transformed for Meena with the arrival of her maternal grand-mother to help the mother after the birth of her second child. Until then India for Meena means little more than the enormous Punjabi meals and Bombay film music which enliven the social gatherings of her parents and their Punjabi friends with possibly the odd reference to Hindu deities and festivals like Diwali. There is a visit to the Sikh temple because the mother is a Sikh who has married a Hindu, a love marriage crossing religious boundaries. Syal provides a few neat touches like this to indicate contemporary Indian secularisms. With the arrival of Nanima, the grandmother, things change. There is a great deal more of the Punjabi language being used in the family, a cultural signifier that Syal appreciates. Nanima and Punjabi friends have a dinner party on their small lawn and Meena hears Punjabi "under the stars". For her it is a revelation as Punjabi "was an indoor language for me, an almost guilty secret which the Elders would only share away from prying English eyes and ears" (ibid. 203). From that point Meena's India widens as she listens to Nanima recounting family gossip and scandal, myths and legends of the Punjab, and begins to be drawn into a world which she has hitherto relegated to the "elders", her parents' generation. Yet, it is mainly an India of the familial, the personalised anecdotes, that engage, and distance, the grandchild.

Syal's novel has been hugely successful in Britain partly through her readings (as a professional actress Syal's performance is superb) and not least because of the narrative's easy resolution of difficult themes such as racism, insularity, a prejudiced neighbourhood that recognises the error of its ignorance. Whether the packaging of India Syal constructs for Meena is a sufficient base for an Indian immigrant girl on which to build secure roots or will be only a part of her identity, (since Meena will also have a British middle-class persona through her grammar school and further academic training) remains open for her readers to decide. What does strike anyone who has admired Syal's brilliant scenario for the gritty realism of the actual lives of a group of Asian women enjoying a day out at the seaside in *Bhaji On The Beach* is the absence of an equally meaningful and less superficial representation of today's India in her novel, which is marred by its desire to present India and Britain in as bland and predictable a manner as possible to please her readers.

The Indian inheritance, regarded with less than enthusiasm when filtered through the interpretations imposed by parents and community, has been affected by the present changes in the lives of Indian women in Britain as well as in India. The second anthology of the Asian Women Writers Collective, (they were renamed by this time), *Flaming Spirit* (Ahmad & Gupta 1994), published six years after their first, reveals a greater concern with women's issues. The heightened consciousness of Asian women in Britain and their fight for equality, opposing racism, sexism and class bias, has made for common ground with sections of the Indian Women's Movement, both fighting for equal rights and contesting Euro-American feminism as white, middle class and preoccupied with women's individualism (Kumar 1993:193-6; Grewal 1988:1-6; Brah 1992).

The intensification of the struggle in India against domestic violence against women, rape and dowry deaths found a sympathetic response from organisations such as Southall Black Sisters, formed in London in 1979 by a group of Asian and African Caribbean women to fight for women's rights and campaign against domestic violence and sexual harassment (1990). That there was a core of common membership in the Asian Women Writers Collective, Southall Black Sisters and Women Against Fundamentalism, formed in 1989, contributed to an ideological receptivity to Indian women's voices raised against the rise of religious fundamentalism in India. After the destruction of Babri Masjid in Ayodhya in 1992, Indian women scholars such as Romila Thapar and Tanika Sarkar were invited to Britain to educate the diaspora about the history of Indian patriarchal traditions and about the growth of the religious right in India.

Circle of Light, the autobiography of Kiranjit Ahluwalia, an Indian woman who killed her husband after suffering physical and mental abuse for ten years, and who would have languished in jail but for the campaign organised by Southall Black Sisters, was written with the help of Rahila Gupta, one of the Asian Writers Collective (Ahluwalia & Gupta 1997). It is an exposé of the notions of *izzat* (honour) harboured by some Asian families in their refusal to support women against violent husbands and other male relations. *Circle of Light* is a landmark in Indian women's autobiographical writing for its honest probing into the cultural background that moulded Kiranjit in India, arranged her marriage and then left her without support to cope with a violent and unstable husband in Britain. It is a book which needs close study to understand the ambivalence with which Indian patriarchal family norms of behaviour are regarded in India, and in Britain by sections of the female diaspora of Indian origin.

The subversion of such norms through irony and satire had begun earlier with the work of Suniti Namjoshi, poet and fabulist, who makes no secret of her lesbianism. In her fables she exposes male hypocrisy by reworking fairy tales, Greek and Sanskrit mythology, and subverting the iconic role of animals such as the cow and the monkey in the Hindu tradition (1981 & 1985). She wonders whether she does commit heresy by inventing gods and goddesses and creating her own stories about them. "Do I blaspheme? I'm not entirely sure how a Hindu might blaspheme or what might constitute a Hindu heresy..." she asks in her latest work, *Building Babel* (1996).

Acculturation, not necessarily linked to feminism, is affecting the gradual marginalisation of India, if not in women's psyche and sense of self, then in their writing. Two examples of women from Indian families who are among the most talented of the younger generation illustrate this new trend.

The publication of a first novel, *Transmission,* by Atima Srivastava in 1992 saw the beginning of a new relationship between the Indian diaspora in Britain and the Indian past. Though the daughter of two well known Hindi poets who have lived in London for the last thirty years and a woman who visits India regularly, Atima Srivastava's writing reveals a new space for the British Asian. Whether such a space can be defined as the assimilated multiculturalism of London or the writer's cosmopolitan outlook cannot be decided. What does stand out is Srivastava's distance from her Indian inheritance. Her first work, a short story that won an award, "Dragons in E. 8" (1995), bears not a single reference to the author's Indian origins. It is narrated by an English girl, a drug addict, who may not have long to live. She is devoid of self-pity while she plans a future with optimistic courage. Srivastava's novel, *Transmission* (1992a), has an Indian woman narrator and occasional allusions to her family. Beyond that the novel charts unfamiliar terrain for Indian or diasporic writing. The narrative focuses on the tension generated in the life of the narrator, a film editor by profession. She falls in love with an English working-class man she had known at school. He is now HIV positive. A modern tragedy, *Transmission* is a study of the urban jungle of the electronic media and cut-throat business ethics of the Thatcher era. As Srivastava said in an interview:

> I don't want to create stereotypical Indian characters that come across as victims, as having been disabled by racism. I wanted to confront the

Thatcher legacy, the power of money, the lack of any proper value system... (1992b)

As the process of acculturation continues despite ethnic minority efforts to resist it or to restrict it to the world outside the family, a younger
generation of British Asian writers is emerging whose connection with
the Subcontinent, with their parental homelands, is scarcely visible. The
Indian part of their cultural hybridity, or the intermediate space between
their Indian and British selves has been eliminated. Their education and
upbringing have been so geared to a native British model that the Indian
connection is no longer needed or missed. With the youngest author of
Indian origins in Britain, we find the real world of the assimilated. Bidisha,
whose surname, Bandyopadhyay, has been dropped by her for her first
novel, *Seahorses* (1997), began her writing career while at school, attracted
the attention of publishers, and has had her novel published while only
19, a student at Oxford University. A hyphenated identity has been dropped
in the publisher's blurb where she is described as British since what she
has written is so removed from diasporic fiction or women's writing as to
be quite unusual. *Seahorses* is the story of three Englishmen, in their thir-
ties, as they pursue their sexual adventures. White middle-class males, the
chosen subject of a Bengali girl's first novel, if it is a pointer to the future,
shows the Indian connection to be neither an inheritance nor a hindrance.
It has ceased to exist.

NOTES

1. For hybridity see Bhabha, Homi, *The Location Of Culture*, London:
   Routledge. 1994, 207-09; for a new Afro-Caribbean/Asian identity,
   identified as black or in some other way, see Modood, Tariq et al (eds.)
   Ethnic Minorities in Britain, London: Policy Studies Institute, 1997: 290-
   97.
2. Markandaya, Kamala, Personal communication, 8th July, 1992.

REFERENCES

Ahluwalia, Kiranjit and Gupta Rahila, *Circle of Light,* London: Harper Collins, 1997.
Ahmad, Rukhsana and Gupta Rahila (eds.), *Flaming Spirit: Stories from the Asian Women Writers' Collective,* London: Virago, 1994.
Ash, Ranjana Sidhanta, "Sujata Bhatt", *P.N. Review* 21. 7. 1995.
Asian Women Writers' Workshop, *Right of Way: Prose and Poetry,* London: Women's Press, 1988.
Bhatt, Sujata, "Search for my Tongue", *Brunizem,* Manchester: Carcanet, 1988.
Bhatt, Sujata, "Buffaloes", *Brunizem*, Manchester: Carcanet, 1988.
Bhatt, Sujata, "Red August". *Monkey Shadows*, Manchester: Carcanet, 1991.
Bidisha, *Seahorses,* London: Flamingo. 1997.
Brah, Avtar, "Difference, Diversity, Differentiation", in Donald, J.& Rattansi, A. (eds), *Race, Culture and Difference,* London: Sage, 1992.
Chatterjee, Debjani and Islam, Rashida, (eds.) *Barbed Lines,* Sheffield: Bengali Women's Support Group and Yorkshire Art Circus, 1990.
Sweet and Sour, Sheffield: Bengali Women's Support Group, 1993.
Coppola, C. (ed.), *Marxist Influences and South Asian Literature,* 2 Vols. East Lansing: Asian Studies Center, 1974.
Dhingra, Leena, *Amritvela*, London: Women's Press, 1988.
Dhingra, Leena, "Breaking Out Of The Labels" in Cobham, R. and Collins, M. (eds.), *Watchers and Seekers,* London: Women's Press, 1987.
Dyson, Ketaki Kushari, *Noton Noton Paayraguli*, novel in Bengali, Calcutta: Ananda Pubs, 1980.
Dyson, Ketaki Kushari, *Spaces I Inhabit,* Calcutta: Navana, 1983.
Dyson, Ketaki Kushari, "Forging a Bilingual Identity: A Writer's Testimony", in Burton, P. et al. (eds.), *Bilingual Women,* Oxford: Berg, 1994.
Grewal, S. et al (eds.), *Charting The Journey: Writings by Black and Third World Women,* London: Sheba, 1988.
Gupta, Sunetra, *Memories of Rain,* London: Orion, 1992.
Gupta, Sunetra, *The Glassblower's Breath,* London: 1993.
Gupta, Sunetra, *Moonlight Into Marzipan,* London: Phoenix House, 1995
Holmstrom, Lakshmi (ed.), *The Inner Courtyard: Stories by Indian Women,* London: Virago, 1990.
Hosain, Attia, *Phoenix Fled*, London: Chatto and Windus, 1953 rep. Virago, 1988a.

Hosain, Attia, *Sunlight On A Broken Column,* London: Chatto and Windus, 1961 rep.Virago, 1988b.

Hosain, Attia. "Second Thoughts". *Independent.* 18th. Aug. 1988c.

Husain, Shahrukh, "Indian Women Writers in Britain and America – Novels on the Asian Experience: Journeys to the Promised Land", unpublished paper, London University: Institute of Commonwealth Studies, 1990

Kumar, Radha, *The History of Doing: An Illustrated Account of Movements for Women's Rights and Feminism in India, 1800-1990,* London: Verso, 1993

Markandaya, Kamala, *Some Inner Fury,* London: Putnam, 1955.

Markandaya, Kamala, *The Coffer Dams,* London: Hamish Hamilton, 1969.

Markandaya, Kamala, *Two Virgins,* New York: John Day, 1973.

Markandaya, Kamala, *The Nowhere Man,* London: Alan Lane, 1973.

Markandaya, Kamala, "One Pair of Eyes: Some Random Reflections", in Niven, A. (ed.), *Commonwealth Writers Overseas: Themes of Exile and Expatriation,* Liege: Didier, 1976.

Markandaya, Kamala, *Pleasure City,* London: Chatto and Windus, 1982.

Markandaya, Kamala, *Nectar In A Sieve,* New York: Signet, 11th imp., 1982, (first pub. 1954).

Namjoshi, Suniti, *Feminist Fables,* London: Sheba, 1981.

Namjoshi, Suniti, *The Conversations of Cow,* London: 1985.

Namjoshi, Suniti, *Building Babel,* North Melbourne: Spinifex Press, 1996.

Randhawa, Ravinder, *A Wicked Old Woman,* London: Women's Press, 1987.

Sahgal, Gita, "Secular Spaces: The Experience of Asian Women Organizing", in Sahgal, G. and Davis, Nira Yuval (eds.), *Refusing Holy Orders: Women and Fundamentalism in Britain,* London: Virago, 1992.

Southall Black Sisters, *Against the Grain: A Celebration of Survival and Struggle, 1979-89.* Southall: SBS Collective, 1990.

Srivastava, Atima, *Transmission,* London: Serpents Tail, 1992a.

Srivastava, Atima, "Interview with Ian Rashid", *Bazaar,* 21, 1992b.

Srivastava, Atima, "Dragons in E 8", *Kunapipi,* XVII. 3, 1995.

Syal, Meera, *Anita and Me,* London: Flamingo, 1996.

Wilson, Amrit, *Finding a Voice: Asian Women in Britain,* London: Virago, 1978.

FORGET INDIA, WE'RE BRITISH!

FELICITY HAND
Universitat Autònoma de Barcelona

Hard-working, law-abiding, locked into their own culture but harmless is the description that comes to mind to many white British people about the Asian[1] community in the United Kingdom. Other Britons may regard them with more suspicion as volatile fundamentalists who refuse to integrate into mainstream culture. Whichever image one has of British people of South Asian descent, it is undeniable that in a relatively short time they have managed to carve themselves a niche in Britain and have contributed to the redefinition of what it means to be British in the post-colonial era. As a detailed anthropological or sociological study is beyond the scope of this article I propose to sketch a brief history of the British Asian community and suggest that Indianness has indeed become an essential part of contemporary Britain.

Hooded Hordes

> Who are those hooded hordes swarming
> Over endless plains ...
> (*The Waste Land*, ll. 369-70)

There have been people of Indian origin in Britain ever since the seventeenth century, coinciding with the establishment of the East India Company in India. Apart from a small number of professional, educated Indians, the majority of these Asians were servants, sailors or people from a low social class, which reinforced the stereotype of the Indian as a servile, obsequious, inferior creature. Prior to World War II, the number of people in Britain of Asian origin was too small for them to qualify as a community. The postwar boom in industry revived the British economy and created a desperate shortage of labour. News of the prosperity and opportunities available in Britain found its way to the Indian subcontinent, acting as a strong pull factor. At the same time, increasing pressure on the land following the partition of India impelled many men to emigrate to seek better conditions abroad. A tradition of migration was quickly established and by the end of the sixties there were already over 50,000 Indians and Pakistanis in Britain (Fryer, 1989:373 & Walvin, 1984:111).

At first the stay in Britain was seen as a temporary measure. On the migrants' return, with the help of their savings, they would sponsor the journey of the next member of the family to go, or else return to Britain themselves after a few years in the subcontinent. After the tightening up of immigration laws enshrined in the Commonwealth Immigrants Acts of 1962 and 1968, the men could not risk taking a prolonged return to the subcontinent to visit their families as they might not be eligible for re-entry into Britain. Primary immigration from India, Pakistan (and the Caribbean), that is the entry of single migrants or heads of households, was destined to virtually come to an end with the passing of the 1971 Immigration Act, making it only possible for dependants to enter the country. Thus many migrants opted for family reunification and women from India, Pakistan and Bangladesh (after 1971) started to arrive in Britain in the sixties and seventies and the establishment of a permanent Asian community in the UK became a reality.

These women often arrived with young children, which tied them to the home. It must also be remembered that many of the early migrants came from rural areas where tradition strongly disproved of women working outside the home. Therefore the Asian women who arrived in Britain during the sixties and seventies hardly came into contact with the indigenous British population. Likewise, the women's presence acted as a reminder to the men, who had migrated earlier, of their Asian cultural values, about which some had become lax. They looked inwardly to their families instead of outwardly to the native population, so, in a sense, the women caused a rupture of relations, whenever they had been established, between male Asians and the white population at large. Apart from the distinctive turbans worn by the Sikhs, Asian men did not dress very differently from British men. On the other hand, the women stood out because of their traditional form of dress. By continuing to wear saris and shalwar kameez and open sandals in the chilly, damp British weather, the women were seen as oddities who were refusing to conform to the British way of life. In a sense the women were feared even more than the men, which is itself an irony considering the well-worn stereotype of the meek and subservient Asian woman, but she was seen as a carrier and transmitter of alien cultural values. This explains why many Asian women were accused of failing to integrate into British society, but their Oriental dress was often merely the outward indication of their seclusion from the Western concept of social integration.

The arrival of the women meant that in time a new phenomenon would arise: the birth of Asian children in Britain. The fears aroused by a significant increase in non-white births were doubtlessly kindled by the realization that many, if not all, of the migrants were here to stay. Uprooting children born and brought up in Britain would be difficult and might easily be postponed until they had completed their schooling, by which time the parents would have become accustomed to the advantages of living in the West and they themselves would be reluctant to leave. Fears of Britain being "swamped" by people of a different culture have proved, however, to be unfounded and inspired by election demagoguery[2]. Statistically speaking, South Asian people are younger on average than white people because of the youth of the early migrants and the fact that they had relatively large families. Although the birth rate is declining among the British-born generation, the British Asian community may easily double its present size in the next twenty or thirty years, but this would still only account for less than 6 percent of the total population of the UK. Naturally, the national average fails to reflect the fact that South Asians are heavily concentrated in London, the industrial Midlands, Yorkshire and the North-West.

The second generation of Asian migrants have had to find a compromise between the two cultures. On the one hand, they have had to succeed in a predominantly white, Christian country, while, on the other hand, their families have wanted them to retain their Asian identity. The third generation, that is the grandchildren of the people who came in the fifties and sixties, many of whom are now young adults, have the advantage of, at least, their parents' understanding of the difficulties of being a Brown Briton. Rather than fall back on the cliché of British Asians being "torn between two cultures", I prefer to adopt Roger Ballard's term of "skilled cultural navigators" (1994:31) to describe the experience of young British Asians. Nevertheless, as Ballard points out, despite their skill in switching cultural codes of behaviour as required, Britons of Asian descent still face all kinds of dilemmas basically because of the mutual distrust, bordering on overt hostility, that persists between the Asians and the white British (ibid. 32).

Ruth Frankenburg and Lata Mani define "post-colonial" in British terms as the "loss of most ... former colonies ... [,] the appearance on British landscapes of a significant number of people from the former colonies ... [and the] transition from a society of predominantly white ethnic groups to one that is multiracial" (1993:292). The extremely conservative part of contemporary Britain may stubbornly cling to the nostalgic but erroneous notion that prior to World War II Britain was a racially homogeneous society, and that the black presence in British cities is not contributing to the redefinition of Britishness, but this is denying the evidence that Britain has lost its position as a global power, that 3 million people in Britain today have ancestral roots in the former colonies, and that in the words of Hanif Kureishi, "the white British ... have to learn that being British isn't what it was" (1986:38). Just how long it takes to become indigenous is a matter of much speculation. The Irish and the Jews, who were despised and feared just a century ago, are now fully-fledged members of mainstream society, but as Charles Moore so succinctly summarized it, "We want foreigners, so long as their foreignness is not overwhelming" (1991:7).

Post-colonial theory has foregrounded the ambiguities and contradictions inherent in the literature of Third World people who contest colonial discourse in the languages of the former metropolitan centre. Much of this theory has focused on a binary set of power relations involving centres versus peripheries and colonisers versus colonized. These binary oppositions tend to assume that there is such a thing as a stable national location. However, in the case of the Asian community in Britain, as for other peoples of the black diaspora, their present position forces them into an ambiguous state. On the one hand, they may regard their country of origin with a kind of nostalgia as "home", and on the other, they demand recognition as fully-fledged citizens of their country of residence. The distance, not only physical but often cultural, between the countries of origin and residence both weakens and strengthens their emotional ties to a lost homeland. Treated as Westerners in India, they have literally been **seen** as aliens in Britain, their skin colour acting as a powerful signifier of the Other. The diasporic person occupies a kind of "Third Space", neither here nor there, but capable of adapting her/himself according to necessity. This concept of hybridity, now most often associated with Homi Bhabha's theories, requires a sense of new identity that can encompass all three: Asian, British, and British Asian. It is in this hybrid sense that British Asian writers or film makers are post-colonial. We still have a long way to go before, in the main, non-white writers can go beyond their ethnicity and just write purely imaginatively because in general they still feel

FELICITY HAND: FORGET INDIA, WE'RE BRITISH! 113

a degree of responsibility to make certain ethnic experiences public knowledge (Hand, 1995:79-80). I would argue that women's experiences are among those that still need to be made known since diaspora cultures tend to normalize the male experience and hide away female accounts of displacement and alienation (Clifford, 1994). It is for this reason that Gurinder Chadha's film *Bhaji on the Beach* (1994) has had such an enormous impact in Britain and abroad. Britons of Asian descent, especially women, constantly need to compromise between the solidarity and security of *izzat* (family honour) and the restraints and limitations of *sharam* (modesty). This compromise is highlighted in Chadha's film, which is very much a British Asian experience as it focuses on the dilemma of British-born girls of Asian parents who refuse to conform to the accepted mode of meek submissiveness. Although Ginder is physically abused by her husband, she is regarded as the wayward one when she abandons her in-laws' home taking their only grandchild with her. Her husband's family shun her and she only finds support among similarly ill-treated women. She is tempted to return to respectability even though this may involve a renewal of the beatings. The film ends on a note of optimism when her husband's aunt, shocked by the sight of Ginder's bruises, which the girl has carefully hidden, shames the husband in front of his brother and the other women. *Sharam* has its limits in a British context.

The success of *Bhaji on the Beach* proves that Asian writers are not afraid to show the internal conflicts that tradition and custom demand be concealed. Racism against Afro-Caribbeans and domestic violence are singled out in this film as examples of the kind of issues that were kept in a closely guarded ethnic closet, away from the prying eyes of prejudiced whites. A minority community needs to feel itself secure enough amongst the host population before it can air its dirty linen in public. Chadha's film, like Kureishi's *My Beautiful Laundrette*, received several accusations of disloyalty to the community for picking on two of the most taboo subjects among Asians: mixed relationships and separation and divorce (Stuart, 1994 and see also Jamal, 1988). However, it is precisely Chadha's courage in going straight to the root of internal conflicts among Asians and in setting the stage for the resolutions of the characters' emotional and physical problems in Blackpool, the quintessential English seaside resort, that she proves how British her film is. *Bhaji on the Beach* is about juggling identities and learning how to come to terms with the restrictions and latitudes of both British and Asian traditions.

From Begging Bowls to Big Business

On the first anniversary of his arrival at Number 10 Downing Street in 1991, former Prime Minister John Major hosted a dinner for Britain's Asian multimillionaires, "together worth £1.5 billion" (Roy, 1991). No doubt, Major had Asian votes in mind and hoped that by wooing Asian businessmen, a more sympathetic climate could be created for the Conservatives even among working-class, Labour-voting members of their ethnic community. In August of the previous year, *Today* and the *Sun* both reported that there were no less than three hundred Asian millionaires in Britain. *Today* claimed that between them their wealth is £2.6 billion (enough to finance 10% of the defence budget (25 August, 1990) whereas the *Sun* calculated the spending power of Britain's 11.5 million Asians to be in the region of £5 billion (27 August, 1990). The figures quoted may be debatable, but what cannot be overlooked is the growing economic potential of the Asian community in contemporary Britain, a remarkable feat if we consider the obstacles that the Asians have had to overcome.

Prior to the Race Relations Act of 1968, which made it unlawful to discriminate against anyone because of his/her colour, race, ethnic or national origins in employment or housing, non-white applicants for professional or managerial appointments were systematically rejected in favour of white candidates, regardless of suitability to the post concerned. Discrimination in employment encouraged many Asian migrants to set themselves up in small businesses and thus obviate the need to integrate in the white labour market. The late sixties and early seventies saw a large number of Asian shops sprouting almost overnight. These shops were essentially family concerns, staffed by the immediate family and patronised by fellow Asians. There was a definite trend towards self-employment among the Indian and Pakistani communities because owning a business represented independence from the white population and provided a means to self-esteem denied by racist employment practices. In this way, an elaborate infrastructure of ethnic services were established to cater for Asian clients. At first white Britons kept their distance, nor would they have been particularly welcome in the initial stage. However, very soon the Asians became more and more visible behind the counter and more and more indigenous British came to rely on the services of the local Asian shop, open seven days a week and sometimes twelve hours a day. Sheer hard work and long opening hours made these tiny businesses flourish and they have come to form an inseparable part of British culture. In the London area alone, 5,500 of the 7,000 newsagents are owned and run by Asians,

3,000 of whom are Patels (*Today,* 8 October 1990). Bhikhu Parekh, leading political scientist and sociologist, forecast a decade ago that "the Asian
presence in critical areas of the British economy at the turn of the century
is bound to be considerable" (Parekh, 1989: 15).

   Ironically, of course, the Asian corner shop (surely now a British insti-
tution?) was born out of the high motivation to succeed together with the
covert racism that the early settlers had to deal with. Their willingness to
take advantage of the opportunities that were available, often ignored by
the white population, has permitted the growth from a handful of hum-
ble grocery shops to 30,000 CTNs (confectionery, tobacco and newsagents) out of a total of 46,000 in the whole country and the ownership of
70% of Britain's 83,200 independently-owned neighbourhood shops
(Parekh, 1997:65). With half of Britain's retail trade in non-white hands,
Asianness is a very visible part of day-to-day British life. Not only have Asians
transformed the appearance of many British High Streets by opening shops
to cater for their community and the host population, but Indian Sikhs and
Bangladeshis have pioneered Indian cuisine and have created a taste for their
cooking among the whites. So-called "Indian" food has become another
inseparable part of British culture, high and low, ever since Indian seamen,
known as Lascars, left stranded in dockland areas began to establish teahouses
and cafes while waiting for a ship. These very modest places of refreshment
gradually evolved into full-scale restaurants in the post World War II years
and have revolutionized British culinary tastes and habits. The term "Indian" restaurant is the one most popularly used but in fact they are mostly
run by Bangladeshi Sylhetis. There are almost 10,000 all over the country
with a turnover of £1.5 billion, and rare is the Briton who has never delighted his or her tastebuds with a curry. It may also be true to say that many
of the more elderly patrons of Indian restaurants would secretly like to re-
patriate the chefs and waiters who do so much to liven up the monotony of
Anglo-Saxon cuisine. Asians have created a need for an important part of
their culture in Britain, having subtly turned the Indian food market into a
billion-pound trade. It is tempting to regard this takeover of local community life as a kind of cultural colonization. In this respect, social anthropolo-
gist Roger Ballard points to the lesson to be learned from the resourceful-
ness of the migrants from the Indian subcontinent:

> It is precisely the minorities' reluctance to adopt the lifestyles and cul-
> tural conventions of their immediate white neighbours which has en-
> sured that they have not shared their fate (Ballard, 1992:489)

The importance of the Asian network of services cannot be underestimated. As they made themselves self-sufficient and independent of the whites, they closed ranks and made integration, or anglicization, virtually unnecessary. One of the many ironies of postwar immigration from India and Pakistan is that one of the main grievances the white population has against the Asians is their apparent unwillingness to integrate and adopt British customs, whereas their flair for business and dogged determination to succeed in a hostile environment has been spurred on by the social marginality that they experienced from the host population at large. One wonders whether Asian businessmen would ever have prospered so much if the first migrants had not been pushed towards finding an alternative to the British system.

The economic success of large numbers of the British Asian community can almost be seen in terms of a reversal of the colonial situation with Asian businessmen regenerating crippled British industries and providing jobs for white workers. One example would be the revival of Leicester's dying knitwear and hosiery industries by Ugandan Asian entrepreneurs, who created 30,000 new jobs in the process (*The Daily Telegraph* 3 April 1991). Certainly, the unprecedented Diwala celebration party, hosted by the Hinduja brothers, the richest Indian family in Britain and possibly in the world, for the benefit of British businessmen, seemed to herald the shape of things to come. Diwala, the festival of lights, is the traditional Hindu New Year celebration and is essentially an (extended) family affair. The situation was an ironic reversal of the previous status quo, with the former Indian subjects clearly laying down the law and the pound notes.

> It was a telling contrast to historical common perceptions of Anglo-Indian relations to see the British with the begging bowls and the Indians dispensing the money and advice (Wahhab, 1990:17).

While it is true that a combination of strong family ties, sheer hard work and thrift have led to a certain degree of upward class mobility among sectors of the Asian community, I am not suggesting that the three hundred Asian millionaires in Britain today compensate for the harsh statistics that show unemployment among Pakistanis and Bangladeshis to be higher than the national average, housing conditions among them much worse, an over-representation in manual work and an income that is less than half the national average in eighty percent of the cases (Parekh, 1997:68). However, when trying to come to terms with identity politics and questions of deciding just who comes under the umbrella of Britishness, what is more relevant: the prosperity of a small thriving middle class or the impersonal and guilt-producing figures of racial discrimination?

In economic terms, rather than political terms, it could be argued that a certain amount of "colonization" has thus been carried out by the Asians and with hardly any resistance by the British. This much is hinted at in the works of the growing number of Asian writers based in the United Kingdom. Asif, the lodger in Hanif Kureishi's play, *Birds of Passage,* does indeed act the part of neo-colonizer by taking over the house and politely but firmly throwing his former landlord out (Kureishi, 1983). However, it is in Kureishi's film *My Beautiful Laundrette* that the Asians really turn the tables on their former rulers. Played by Daniel Day Lewis, Johnny, the fascist, who once paraded through the streets of Lewisham crying "Immigrants Out", ends up working for his Pakistani school friend, Omar, in his laundrette. The efficient ethnic network, in which members of the extended family are bound to help one another to find their economic feet, has enabled Omar to take his personal revenge on Johnny and his kind:

> I'm not gonna be beat down by this country. When we were at school, you and your lot kicked me all round the place. And what are you doing now? Washing my floor. That's how I like it. Now get to work. Get to work I said. Or you're fired! (Kureishi 1986:92)

Access to the power houses of Britain implies the possibility of subversive manoeuvres from within the system as opposed to mutinous attacks from without. Kureishi's characters speak the language of economic power and, as Omar's uncle, Nassar, tells Johnny, have no time for positive discrimination and Commissions for Racial Equality.

> We're professional businessmen. Not professional Pakistanis. There's no race question in the new enterprise culture (ibid:82).

Kureishi breaks down the stereotyped image of passive Indians, meekly awaiting the hand of British justice. Asif, Nasser and Omar himself have learnt the Thatcherite lesson of self-help better than the Iron Lady's own kith and kin.

One of the legacies of British colonialism, particularly in the Indian subcontinent, was to encourage the fragmentation of the populations along fault-lines of previously dormant senses of difference, thereby discouraging any kind of solidarity. However, the "divide and rule" principle practised by the British in India does not seem to have survived decolonization among the Asian community in Britain. The extent of the Asian communal spirit may, of course, be exaggerated, their patronage and support to fellow Asians being offered out of convenience or necessity (Cashmore, 1991:353), but the rising power of many of Britain's Asians owes a great deal to their strong family ties together with individual hard work and thrift. If Enoch Powell's forebodings are correct and the black man ever does have the whip-hand over the white man[3], the latter will have no-one to blame but himself. The experience of both naked and covert racism have spurred many Asians on to success and the willingness to take advantage of the opportunities that are available, often ignored by the indigenous population (Forester, 1978). Kureishi's Asif in *Birds of Passage* can see that "there's plenty of opportunities for Asians in this country" (37) and while white anti-racist sympathizers are prepared to disrupt a meeting of local anti-black residents, he retorts that:

> ... we don't need your help. We'll protect ourselves against boots with our brains. We won't be on the street because we'll be in cars. We won't be throwing bricks because we'll be building houses with them. They won't abuse us in factories because we'll own the factories and sack people (57).

Paul's sly question as regards who is actually included in Asif's "we", "Will everyone own factories or only those of you with wealthy fathers in Western-supported fascist countries?" (58) does not alter the golden rule of immigrant life in Britain: "you have to make money, that's all" (36).

Hanif Kureishi's film was savagely criticized for pandering to white liberalism. The outrage expressed by Asian people themselves only proves how Asian writers and film makers are still encumbered with the burden of being regarded as representatives of the community. If Kureish's first foray into the movie world was greeted with complaints about its undermining the powerless and diluting Asian identity by some people, and as ultra-conservative by others (Jamal 1988, 22), it will be interesting to see how his new film, *My Son the Fanatic*, will be received. At the time of writing the film was not yet on general release, but it is based on a short story of the same name published in 1996. In this new film Kureishi goes right to the core of British prejudice and fears by presenting a young British-born Asian who becomes a religious zealot. The bitter and violent reaction to *The Satanic Verses*, ostensibly a book that exposes, among other issues, racial discrimination within Britain itself, has sown the seeds for the cultivation of another bogeyman: the Islamic fundamentalist. The uproar over the *fatwa* and the subsequent book burnings has unfortunately distracted public opinion from the harsh facts surrounding job discrimination and racist attitudes in the United Kingdom at the close of the twentieth century. Unemployment among ethnic minorities is still twice as high as for white people and the latter are, on the whole, prepared to admit that racism is the problem (Anwar 1998: 186-7). What is encouraging, and is a sign that the idea of Britishness is gradually expanding to include all British-born people regardless of ethnicity, colour, religion and/or language, is the fact that young Asian people are not accepting second-class citizenship lying down. In the 1990s young Asians are quite confident in asserting their right to equal treatment in education, the labour market and public life. While their parents' or grandparents' cultural origins no longer demand absolute fidelity, they still pay more than just lip-service to their Asianness. However, it is slowly evolving into a new kind of cultural identity, a synthesis, still problematic, of the best of both worlds: Asian and British. As a tribute to the British Asian community I think it is only right to give the last word to a young British Bangladeshi, Poonam Alam, who may not represent her community in any way but who voices the optimism of the younger generation,

> Sometimes, I think I have the best of both worlds but sometimes I think I am not really a part of either. Maybe I am on the outside of both and I cannot be accepted by either unless I let go of the other. But I can never let go without losing part of myself in the process. (Kassam, 1997: 97)

NOTES

1. By "Asian" I am using an umbrella term of convenience to refer to people of Indian, Pakistani and Bangladeshi origin.
2. This of course refers to Margaret Thatcher's notorious speech delivered a year before the Conservatives returned to power in 1979, in which she warned that the present rate of immigration "means that people are really rather afraid that this country might be swamped by people of a different culture. The British character has done so much for democracy, for law, and done so much throughout the world that if there is any fear that it might be swamped, then people are going to be rather hostile to those coming in". *The Guardian,* 31 January 1978.
3. See Powell's infamous "Rivers of Blood" speech of April 20, 1968.

REFERENCES

Anwar, Muhammad, *Between Cultures. Continuity and Change in the Lives of Young Asians*, London: Routledge, 1998.

Ballard, Roger, "New Clothes for the Emperor?: The Conceptual Nakedness of the Race Relations Industry in Britain", *New Community*, Vol. XVIII. No. 3, 1992: 481-492.

Ballard, Roger, "Introduction: the Emergence of *Desh Pardesh*", in *Desh Pardesh: The South Asian Presence in Britain*, ed. Roger Ballard, London: Hurst & Company. 1994

Cashmore, Ellis, "Flying Business Class: Britain's New Ethnic Elite", *New Community*, Vol. XVII, No. 3. 1991: 347-358.

Chadha, Gurinder (dir.), *Bhaji on the Beach*, 1994.

Clifford, James, "Diasporas", *Cultural Anthropology*, Vol. 9, No. 3, 1994: 302-338.

Forester, Tom, "Asians in Business", *New Society*, 23 February 1978: 420-423.

Frankenburg, R. & Mani, L., "Crosscurrents, Crosstalk: Race, "Postcoloniality", and the Politics of Location", *Cultural Studies*, Vol. 7, No. 2, 1993: 292-310.

Fryer, Peter, *Staying Power, The History of Black People in Britain*, London: Pluto Press, 1989.

Hand, Felicity, "A Talk With David Dabydeen", *Links & Letters*, N° 2, 1995: 79-86.

Jamal, Mahmood. "Dirty Linen". in *Black Film British Cinema*. ed. Kobena Mercer. ICA Documents 7. 1988.

Kassam, Nadya (ed). *Telling It Like It Is. Young Asian Women Talk*. London: The Women's Press. 1997.

Kureishi, Hanif, *Birds of Passage*, London: Amber Lane Press, 1983.
    My Beautiful Laundrette and the Rainbow Sign, London: Faber & Faber, 1986.

Kureishi, Hanif, "My Son the Fanatic", in *The Post-Colonial Question*. ed. Iain Chambers & Lidia Curti, London: Routledge, 1996.

Moore, Charles, "Time for a More Liberal and "Racist" Immigration Policy", *The Spectator*, 19 October 1991: 7.

Parekh, Bhikhu, "Asian Aid to Britain", *Asian Enterprise and the Regeneration of Britain*, London: New Life Publication, 1989.

Parekh, Bhikhu, "South Asians in Britain", *History Today*, Vol. 47, No. 9, 1997: 65-68.

Roy, Amrit, "Indian Summer in a Time of Recession", *The Daily Telegraph*, 3 April 1991.

Stuart, Andrea, "Blackpool Illumination", *Sight and Sound*, February 1994: 26-7.

Wahhab, Iqbal, "No Ordinary Diwala Party", *Independent*, 24 October 1990:17.

Walvin, James, *Passage to Britain*, Harmondsworth: Penguin, 1984.

IV

INDIA ON THE MOVE

WHAT BENGAL THINKS TODAY, INDIA THINKS TOMORROW: BANGLA FICTION AND ITS ROLE IN SHAPING THE INDIAN NATIONAL MOVEMENT

SOMDATTA MANDAL

Vivekananda College, University of Calcutta

TO MY NATIVE LAND
My country! in thy days of glory past
A beauteous halo circled round thy brow,
And worshipped as a deity thou wast –
Where is thy glory, where the reverence now?
Thy eagle's pinion is chained down at last,
And grovelling in the lowly dust art thou,
Thy minstrel hath no wreath to weave for thee,
Save the sad story of thy misery!

Well – let me dive into the depths of time,
And bring from out the ages that have rolled
A few small fragments of these wrecks sublime
Which human eye may never more behold;
And let the guardian of my labour be,
My fallen country! One kind wish for thee!

Henry Louis Vivien Derozio (1809-1831) teacher at Hindoo College, Calcutta and the undisputed leader of the Young Bengal Movement.

Historically speaking, British rule in India may be said to have started in 1757 when, at the Battle of Plassey, forces of the British East India Company defeated Sirajuddaula, the Nawab of Bengal. The very nature of British rule resulted in nationalistic sentiments arising among the Indian people and produced the material, moral, intellectual and political conditions for the rise and development of a powerful national movement. Bengal's role in the struggle against British imperialism during the second half of the nineteenth century and the first half of the twentieth need not be reiterated. Keeping in mind Gokhale's famous statement mentioned in the title[1], and the intricate relationship between literature and politics, this paper seeks to trace the history of India's struggle for independence as reflected in the writings of the Bengali intelligentsia and especially through Bangla fiction. Without going into the controversy of how far life imitates art or art imitates life, I would like to trace the various tenets of this movement, showing how ultimately the writers went beyond mere politics to articulate a larger moral-aesthetic vision and that is why their novels are still widely read and appreciated.

All nationalist movements have relied on literature – novelists, singers and playwrights – to hone rallying symbols of past and self through which dignity might be reasserted. As elsewhere in the colonial world, there was a parallel movement between political action and the creation of imaginative literature, of the oppressed moving from silence to intervene in the colonial fictions which presumed to describe them (see Boehmer, 1995). The Bengal scenario was not much different. A survey of historical data and the history of Bangla nationalist literature written in rejection of the Empire shows a firm connection. In 1765, British control in Bengal was firmly established by Robert Clive taking over the revenue management. By 1784, Bengal was placed under the dual control of the East India Company and the British Crown. The Permanent Settlement in Bengal came in 1793. Within a year of the Sepoy Mutiny in 1857, the sovereignty of India was vested in the British monarch through the Government of India Act. The following year witnessed the Indigo Revolt in Bengal. Aukshoy Kumar Dutta's article *Tinattabodhini Patrika* against the oppression by the British indigo planters flowered in a more literary form through Dinabandhu Mitra's drama *Nildarpan,* translated into English by Michael Madhusudan Dutt and published by Reverend James Long, who was both fined and confined for the act. Several articles in journals published from Bengal namely, *Sandhya, Prabashi, Bharati, Bhandar, Nabya-Bharat, Jugantar* and others had already had tremendous impact upon the minds of their readers and inculcated a hidden revolutionary zeal in the common man. The secret report of the British intelligence investigative department was that vernacular papers were propagating extreme anger against British rule. Every year from 1867 to 1880 the Hindoo Mela was held regularly under the auspices of Nabagopal Mitra, Ganendranath Tagore and Dwijendranath Tagore. This mela contributed a great deal to the growth of nationalism in the country.

1876 can be taken as a landmark year for several historical reasons. Bankimchandra Chattopadhyay had composed his song 'Vande Mataram' (which he would later insert in his novel *Anandamath* in 1882). Sivnath Shastri made a small, select band of young patriots take the *Agnimantra* (Oath of Flame). One of the seven pledges taken by them was as follows:

> We consider self-government to be the only form of government that God approves. Yet, considering the present state of the country, we shall abide by the laws of the present government. But whatever poverty, oppression or misery confront us, we shall never accept slavery under the present rulers (Dept. of Information & Cultural Affairs, 1987:49).

The very same year saw the emergence of the *Sanjivani Sabha* (Revival Meeting) under the leadership of Rabindranath Tagore's elder brother Jyotirindranath. Of that meeting, Tagore wrote:

> Jyotidada had set up a secret society. Its sessions were held in a deserted house. Rajnarain Bose was the mentor, sitting there with a skull and copy of the Rig-Veda in front of him. It is there that we took the pledge to liberate India (ibid.)

Such activities during the early nationalist period were part of a wider ideological movement which had autonomy and self-assertion as their watchword, but which also involved sections of the Indian middle classes in processes of self-introspection and cultural retrieval. Bengal especially, was the site of an urgent new nationalism to which Bankimchandra Chattopadhyay, Rabindranath Tagore and others gave a vernacular literary expression. To resist the dilution of indigenous cultures under British rule, Bankim developed Bangla as a narrative medium. Already he had written several historical romances such as *Durgeshnandini*, *Krishnakanter Will* and *Debi Chaudhurani*, used to counter the negative images of colonial rule. In *Anandamath*, the fabulist Bengali retelling of the late eighteenth century resistance to the East India Company, the forests of Bengal are evoked in romantic terms as a type of fragrant Eden. Though the protagonist Satyananda's character is inspired by a grand idealism which is slightly unhistoric, in the novel Bankimchandra incorporates the 'Vande Mataram' anthem and gives it an appropriate context, i.e. a realistic description of a famished country ripe for revolution, a moving story, and certain characters who try to live the message enshrined in the song and the slogan. Coming to more prosaic details, the writer also gives a wonderful outline of the plan and programme which might bind together dedicated patriots and prepare them for guerilla warfare as well as for pitched battles.

Bankimchandra's nationalism, which is reflected in many of his novels, is also urgently and elaborately argued in many of his essays collected in *Anushilan* or *Dharmatattwa* where he makes a subtle distinction between liberty and independence, without any suggestion that any actual political consequences were contemplated. Nevertheless, when a few years later, possibly under Aurobindo Ghosh's direction, young men inspired by patriotic zeal began to give Anushilan and other organizations a revolutionary turn, and Barindrakumar Ghosh established a factory for manufacturing bombs, they probably modelled their organization on Satyananda's Ananda Math and took their idea of manufacturing guns from Bankim's novel. According to Sri Aurobindo, Bankim was more a poet and a prophet than a novelist and he used his fiction as a means of expressing his spiritual thought (Sengupta 1984: 25). He was undoubtedly a contradictory figure. One controversy that Bankimchandra had to face resulted from his in accepting the official title of "Raibahadur", awarded by the British Government on New Year 1892, which seems ironic of the person who composed 'Vande Mataram', inspiring many fearless patriots to mount the gallows with his song on their lips. *Anandamath* has also been criticised for having a religious bias, for upholding the Hindu cause and for being not a historical novel but a novel of 'ideas', expressing a political philosophy that was primarily feudal and idealistic. He appears to have accepted the reality of continuing British rule, and even if he accepted them as enemies, he does not seem to have had the courage to admit it publicly. According to Subodh Sengupta, Bankim "wanted to inculcate patriotism as a religion and present the motherland as a divinity" (ibid: 29).

Rabindranath Tagore's nationalist views, unlike Bankimchandra's, were much more liberal – more open to Western influence and less communal. His first novel, *Bouthakuranir Haat*, published in the same year as *Anandamath*, expressed no comparable nationalist fervour, though his other writings during this time clearly establish the fact that he was still under the influence of the Hindu nationalist group. But his novels are more acutely connected to the turbulent intellectual currents of this period in Indian history, and as such Tagore played a crucial role in both reflecting and moulding the intellectual, social and cultural climate in a resurgent Bengal. Convinced of the decadence of Indian culture, he responded readily to the rationalistic, humanistic and literary influences of the West, and ushered in a new era in Bangla literature. After the division of Bengal in 1905 and with the rise of the *Swadeshi* movement and boycott of foreign goods, he could not keep himself totally away from the clash between reformist and revitalist forces – the conflict between moderate and extremist elements in politics as well as the eternal struggle in the human consciousness between love and sacrifice[2].

Tagore decried the popular brand of patriotism, based on emotionalism and chauvinism and held that independence was best achieved not by the denunciation of the British and violent agitation against them but by the promotion of self-help and strength. A weak India without self-sufficiency and social freedom was not fit to govern itself, and neither grandiose talk nor violence, but only sacrifice and service were the true tests of strength. Two novels, *Ghare-Baire (The Home and the World)* and *Char-Adhyay (Four Chapters)* embody the above theme, though the main interest in both is in the human rather than the political situation. Nikhil and, to a certain extent, Bimala in the first novel, and the two lovers, Ela and Atin, in the second, face suffering and tragedy by being caught up in the convulsions of the political struggle. The novel *Gora* upholds the ideal of the synthesis of races, religions and cultures which Tagore was never tired of proclaiming. Starting as a fanatically orthodox and xenophobic Hindu, Gora moves, urged on by his disillusioning experiences and the final revelation of his true identity, towards the goal of liberal cosmopolitanism and the ideal of India as a centripetal civilization. His other novels such as *Chokher Bali (Binodini)*, *Nauka Dubi (The Wreck)*, and *Chaturanga* relate to some of the pressing social issues which rocked Bengali Hindu society towards the end of the last century.

According to the historian Sumit Sarkar (Sarkar, 1973), the Indian nationalist movement can roughly be divided into four categories, namely (a) the movement initiated by people like Surendranath Banerjee, who were much more liberal and kept the revolution confined within certain limits, such as the boycott of goods etc.; (b) the constructive Swadeshis who emphasized self-confidence, national integration, national education of the masses; (c) the extremists who wanted to turn the boycott into a revolutionary upheaval but without bloodshed and through passive resistance; (d) the anarchists and revolutionaries who wanted an armed struggle, to kill the imperialist rulers and create upheaval in the country. Though many of these sections overlapped, Tagore essentially supported the second point of view, with certain reservations of his own. His nationalism was more concerned with exploring social issues against the backdrop of nationalist ones. In his fiction, taking India as the backdrop, he tried to explore universal human motivations at "home". He remained, for the most part, a believer in the utopian hope of social justice through the enlightened, humanitarian efforts of the "natural" leaders of society, who were for him the *zamindars*[3.] However, Nikhil in *Ghare Baire*, though coming closest to this moral ideal, remains ineffectual and is possibly killed. Though Lukacs seems to me mistaken in his assessment of the novel[4], this incident is perhaps an indication of Tagore's personal uncertainties about a social system visibly on the decline[5]. The alternative figure is Sandip, the outsider, who is an anarchist, and who boldly declares, "I shall simply make Bimala one with my country" (Tagore, 1985). It has to be remembered, of course, that this novel belongs to a pre-Gandhian and ideologically far more troubled era in the history of Indian nationalism. Following the Jalianwallabagh massacre and his rejection of a knighthood, Tagore lent his support to the Gandhian credo of non-violence and constructive work, declaring in bold terms, "I refuse to waste my manhood in lighting the fire of anger and spreading it from house to house" (Mukhopadhyay in Chowwdhury 1983:60). His last novel, *Char Adhyay (Four Chapters)* published in 1933, projects his theme of the tragic dialectic between political agitation and human values. Questioning blind nationalism and blind adherence to leaders, Tagore cautions the reader against paying undue critical attention to the setting of the story, the terrorist movement in Bengal, at the expense of the story itself[6]. The British used the novel against the nationalist movement, other forms of political activity and the poet himself. Moreover, Ela's willing renunciation of militancy in favour of a domestic role may be taken as patriarchal wish-fulfilment on the part of her creator, who was aware of women's increasing participation in militant politics in the 1930s. Asserting the continuing relevance of Tagore's ideas, Kumar Sahani, who recently adapted the novel into film, told *India Today* (July 14, 1997:92) that Tagore's totally different ideas about nationalism motivated him to make the film. "The novel was written in Kandy and already Tagore was moving towards a pan-Asiatic internationalistic vision", he says. Though the book does not have a clearly defined narrative, Sahani thought that it expressed Tagore's credo effectively. "He believed in the right to self-determination, self-realization, which was higher than any ethnicised concept of nationalism".

II

This brief survey of nationalist Bangla fiction shows one point very clearly, that each individual writer propounded his own individual beliefs and political faith. The differences between the novels of Tarashankar Bandodaphyay and Sharat Chandra Chattopadhyay exemplify this. Chronologically speaking, though he started writing later than Sharat Chandra, Tarashankar's writings propound a rather similar vision of a feudal aristocratic society as in the novels of Bankimchandra, though as a true Congressman and a Gandhian, his vision shows a shift in focus from Bankim's. By the time he started writing, British imperialism had spread its tentacles so far that it was much easier for him to consider the British as enemies. But, like Bankim, he did not support any form of social revolution that would harm the educated middle class. In other words, even though the British were his enemies, he was not on the side of the ordinary people. Though his first novel, *Chaitali Ghurni* (*The Cyclone*), depicts the conflict between the rulers and the ruled, namely the zamindars versus the peasants, the treatment of this theme is without any revolutionary implication. With *Dhatri Devata* (*Mother Earth*), things become more concrete when its protagonist, Shibnath, reveals nationalistic ideals much in the line of Ananda Math. As the active involvement of the ordinary people in the nationalist movement increased, Tarashankar turned his focus from the zamindars to the peasants in his later novels such as *Ganadebata* (*Lord of the People*) and *Panchagram* (*Five Villages*).

Sharat Chandra Chattopadhyay was a reformist from the beginning of his career who assumed that the time would come when the British would have to leave the country. Unlike Tagore, who was primarily a poet and philosopher, Sharat Chandra was a professional Bengali novelist whose novels reveal much more explicitly the social and cultural ethos of the time. Entering active politics in 1921, when the influence of Gandhi's non-cooperation movement was growing, Chattopadhyay's desire for India's freedom stemmed from the social tragedy which he saw all around him. After the Chauri-Chaura incident of 1922 and the imprisonment of Gandhi, he regretted that Bengal lacked the capacity and opportunity for organised violence. In 1926, his revolutionary approach expressed itself in his firebrand novel *Pather Dabi* (*Demand of the Road*). This novel became the "scripture" of contemporary revolutionaries and within a few days of its publication, the British government seized the book. Without punishing the author or the publisher, they merely banned its circulation, only lifted after the writer's death[7]. Considering the active revolutionary path propagated by Sabyasachi, the protagonist of the novel, and also the views expressed in other articles and letters, it becomes clear that till the end Sharat Chandra never really reconciled the conflicting attractions of reformist non-violence and revolutionary armed struggle. It is evident, though, that the Russian Revolution influenced his views. *Charitraheen* (*Characterless*), for example, depicts his distaste for the bourgeoisie as does his incomplete *Jagaran* (*The Awakening*).

By the 1930s, Bengal was a Marxist bastion. In 1937, there was the largest struggle of the working class in the jute workers general strike which lasted for 74 days. The emergence of writers such as Manik Bandopadhyay who proclaimed himself an active member of the Communist Party of India was part of this ferment. Rejecting the reformist nationalism of Tarashankar, Manik felt that the liberation of the country would not change the economic circumstances of the proletariat. What he wanted was a socialist state which totally uprooted the institutions of the imperial regime[8]. Using language as a tool of protest, his novels *Sahartali* (*The Suburbs*), *Pratibimba* (*The Reflection*), *Ahimsa* (*Non-Violence*), *Darpan* (*The Mirror*) reveal his socialist leanings quite clearly. So too does Satinath Bhaduri's *Jagori* which deals with the tribulations of a revolutionary political prisoner facing his imminent death sentence.

Throughout the several phases of India's nationalist movement, there have been significant works of Bangla literature which express the political currents of their time. Having recently celebrated the golden jubilee of India's independence, it is interesting to note that this radical political tradition in the Bangla novel is still very much alive. Samaresh Basu's *Tin Purush* (*Three Generations*), Unil Gangopadhyay's *Purba-Paschim* (*East/West*) and *Pratham Alo* (*First Light*) (which is currently being serialized in a leading Bangla literary magazine), show that there is a strong tradition within Bangla literature which regards the core of the political struggle as not so much that between the colonial power and its nationalist opponents, but between the native elite and the group the sociologist Ranajit Guha has simply called "the people" (Ranajit, 1988:44).

From this brief survey of Bangla fiction and the various nuances of its nationalist stance, it becomes clear that, though any piece of writing is a product of its time, the best writing overcomes its immediate political credo and expresses a state of tension, leading towards what Irving Howe aptly calls the "apolitical" element. Indeed, Howe's definition of the political novel seems particularly pertinent to the heterogeneous arena of Bangla political fiction:

> For both the writer and the reader, the political novel provides a particularly severe test.... For the writer, the great test is, how much truth can he force through the sieve of his opinions? For the reader, the great test is, how much of that truth can he accept though it jostle his opinions?..... It is not surprising that the political novelist, even as he remains fascinated by politics, urges his claim for a moral order beyond ideology; nor that the receptive reader, even as he preserves his own commitment, assents to the novelist's order (Howe, 1970:25-6).

NOTES

1. R.K.Dasgupta, eminent scholar and former director of the National Library at Calcutta, contends that economic swadeshi deserves commemoration, at least in West Bengal, because its first exponents were Bengalis. In a letter to the editor, dated 4th September 1997, he states, "While I say this I quote the words which we put into the mouth of Gopal Krishna Gokhale because, I think, he never spoke them – 'What Bengal thinks today, the rest of India thinks tomorrow'. What Gokhale actually said as president of the twenty-first session of the Indian National Congress held in Benaras in 1905 is "what the educated Indians think today, the rest of India thinks tomorrow" (quoted in Annie Besant, *How India Wrought for Freedom* 1915; 2nd ed. 1975: 421). It is, however, true that Gokhale was full of praise for Bengal in this presidential address where he said: "the public life in this country has received an accession of strength, and for this all India owes a deep debt of gratitude to Bengal". This was said in appreciation of the Swadeshi Movement, which had begun in Bengal a few months earlier. *The Statesman*, 12 September 1997:8.

2. Tagore upholds this point of view in *The Home and the World* by contrasting the political actions of his two male protagonists, Nikhil and Sandip. Sandip's aggressive individualism translates into the disruptive practices of terrorism. According to Nikhil, the *swadeshi* youths, all products of colonial education, remain alienated from the peasant masses they profess to want to liberate. Nikhil categorically denounces the political philosophy of revolutionary terrorism as a psychological legacy of colonial domination: "you have been so used to submit to domination, you have come to believe that to make others submit is a kind of religion", he says (174). On this issue one might recall Tagore's own views on extremism, clearly articulated in the essay "Nationalism in India" (1917), where he charged that the goal of the extremists was "based on Western history" and that they had failed to understand the root causes of India's suffering: its history of caste and religious antagonisms. (*Nationalism*, London: Macmillan, 1917.)

3. For more details see Mitra, Indrani, "I Will Make Bimala One With My Country": Gender and Nationalism in Tagore's *The Home and the World*", *Modern Fiction Studies* 41, 2, Summer 1995: 243-264.

4. Lukacs, Georg, "Tagore's Gandhi Novel: Review of Rabindranath Tagore: *The Home and the World*", *Reviews and Articles* from *Die Rote Fahne,* Trans. Peter Palmer, London: Merlin Press, 1983:8-11. Lukacs'

misinterpretation reads as follows: "Tagore himself is, as imaginative writer and as thinker, a wholly insignificant figure. His creative powers are non existent; his characters pale stereotypes; his stories threadbare and uninteresting; and his sensibility is meagre, insubstantial... The hypothesis is that India is an oppressed, enslaved country, yet Mr. Tagore shows no interest in this question".

5. Taraknath Das in *Rabindranath Tagore – His Religious, Social and Political Ideals* (Calcutta, 1932:51) illustrates this point in details: "Rabindranath possesses a double personality, however dynamic it may be. When he visits western countries and on his return addresses the people here (in India), his poetic sensitive soul is enraptured by the energy of the life in the west, its freedom, expansiveness and her magnificent works of art. When he stays in India for a sufficiently long time to intensely feel with a subject race (his own people, his kith and kin) what western man has made of man in India, his rebellious spirit flares up in righteous indignation".

6. Raj, G.V., *Tagore: The Novelist,* New Delhi: Sterling Publishers, 1983: 96. That Tagore brought Ela from the radical political arena back into the domestic one in *Char Adhyay* is meant to convince his readers of the utter futility of the terrorist path as a means of attaining the country's freedom. In two essays of the time entitled "Path O Prakreya" ("The Way and the Means") and "Samasya" ("The Problem"), he argued that the radical political activities in the *swadeshi* period were all attempts at short cuts: "Just because I am in a hurry", he wrote, " the road does not shorten". Also see Leonard A Gordon, *Bengal: The Nationalist Movement 1876-1940,* New Delhi: Manohar Book Service, 1974: 157-58. Also see Sinha, Sasadhar, *Social Thinking of Rabindranth Tagore,* Bombay: Asia Pub. House, 1962.

7. Sri Charubikash Dutta and Sri Surya Sen were the supreme commanders of the Chittagong Youth Revolt during 1930-1934 in which a group of young revolutionaries captured two armories in the town, disconnecting Chittagong's link with the outside world. According to Charubikash's memoirs, Sharat Chandra's *Pather Dabi* was published when they were absconding and trying to evade arrest, under the Bengal Ordnance, by living in hidden dens. Reading of Sabyasachi's revolutionary life and character had a great impact upon their lives then, inspiring them to such an extent that whenever the novel was read and discussed, Surya Sen would remain entranced for a long time. (See Nazma Jasmine Chowdhury, 1983:107.) Tagore's criticism of the novel

was based on the fact that he considered it not as a work of art but as an anti-imperialist treatise in the guise of a story. Sharat Chandra, of course, remained firm in his point of view, "No one can prevent the onslaught of youth-power, which is seeking avenues to express itself".

8. Manik Bandopadhyay emphasized class-struggle and probably was the first Bengali novelist to focus his work upon the struggles of the peasant class. A true Marxist, discarding the idea of religion, the one belief that runs through his political novels is that permanent peace and beauty can never be attained.

9. For further details see Gangopadhyay, Sunil, *Shei Shomoy* (translated into English by Aruna Chakravarti as *Those Days: A Novel,* New Delhi: Penguin India, 1997). Though the novel focuses on the Bengal Renaissance between the decades 1840 to 1870, there are hints suggesting that apart from being an era of enlightenment, this period was also the seeding time of nationalistic fervour that culminated in the *Swadeshi* Movement later on. Though he does not offer the final answer, Gangopadhyay maintains that history in the conventional sense is not central to his metier.

REFERENCES

Boehmer, Elleke, *Colonialist and Post Colonial Literature,* New York: Oxford UP, 1995.

Department of Information & Cultural Affairs, Govt. of West Bengal, *India's Struggle for Freedom: An Album,* 1987.

Chowdhury, Nazma Jasmine, *Bangla Uponyas O Rajniti*, Calcutta: Chirayat Prakashan, 1983.

Guha, Ranajit, "On Some Aspects of the Historiography of Colonial India", *Selected Subaltern Studies,* Eds. Ranajit Guha and Gayatri Chakravorty Spivak, New York: Oxford Univ. Press, 1988.

Howe, Irving, *Politics and the Novel,* (1957), New York: Avon, 1970.

Mukhopadhyay, Prabhatkumar, *Rabindra Jiboni,* Vol.III, 1946, in Chowdhury, Nazma Jasmine, *Bangla Uponyas O Rajniti*, Calcutta: Chirayat Prakashan, 1983.

Sarkar, Sumit, *Swadeshi Movement in Bengal: 1903-1905,* New Delhi: People's Publishing House, 1973.

Sengupta, Subodh, *Swami Vivekananda & Indian Nationalism,* Calcutta: Sahitya Samsad, 1984.

Tagore, Rabindranath, *The Home and the World,* Trans. by Surendranath Tagore, (1919), Macmillan India, 1985.

THE PEACOCK PRESS – INDIAN MEDIA IN AN AGE OF GLOBALISATION

DAYA THUSSU
Coventry University, UK

Introduction

This chapter surveys the evolution of the media in independent India, as the country celebrates the golden jubilee of its independence from British colonial rule. It examines the challenges and opportunities that globalisation has opened up for media industries in India and analyses policy initiatives of the Indian government in response to globalisation.

The first part of the chapter locates the current debates about the identity of the Indian media within the historical context of its evolution. It then examines the role of the media as a fourth estate in India, where the past 50 years of multi-party polity have ensured the freedom of the media in the world's largest democracy. India has one of the world's largest press systems, with nearly 4,000 dailies and some 24,000 magazines published in 80 languages.

The chapter argues that after independence, the media saw itself as playing an important role in "nation building". A consensus evolved under which the privately-owned press had freedom to critically engage with issues of national import while the electronic media was used by the state as an instrument of mass persuasion. The system worked more or less well as long as India was governed by the powerful Congress Party, which had led the anti-colonial movement. But by the 1970s that consensus was under strain as the Congress was weakened and regional parties gained ascendancy, contributing to the growth of an oppositional discourse in the media and the growth of the Indian language press.

The final part of the chapter will analyse how the economic liberalisation of India, under globalisation, has affected the traditional mainstream media. It will examine whether the expansion of Western media conglomerates threatens the diversity and vitality which has characterised the Indian media since its inception or offers new opportunities. The chapter examines the policy choices of the Indian government as it tries to change the country's media industries to adjust to the competitive, deregulated and privatised environment of the late 1990s.

The Historical Context

To have a better understanding of the media in contemporary India, it is important to examine its evolution. From the advent of newspaper publishing in India with the *Bengal Gazette* in 1780[1], newspapers acted as a harbinger of modernity, contributing significantly to the construction of a national identity. Despite very low literacy and strict press laws introduced by successive British colonial administrations, the press played a key role in the nationalist movement, even if its pioneers came from a small Westernised, educated elite.

Such was Ram Mohan Roy, a versatile Bengali intellectual, who established the nationalist press in India in the early 1820s by starting three reformist publications – the *Brahmanical Magazine*, in English, the *Sambad Kaumudi* in Bengali, and the *Mirat-ul-Akhbar* in Persian. At the same time, at the other end of the country, Fardoonji Murzban launched the *Bombay Samachar* in 1822, which as a Gujarati daily is still in existence. (Rau, 1974: 22)

Roy's contemporary, Lord William Bentinck, a relatively liberal Governor General, supported Indian efforts at reforms and, as a result, by 1830 there were already 33 English language and 16 Indian language publications in operation. In subsequent decades many more nationalist newspapers and magazines appeared. Among the key publications were *Rast Goftar*, edited by Dadabhai Naoroji, the founder of the Indian National Congress, and *Shome Prakash*, in Bengali, started in 1858 by Iswar Chandra Vidyasagar.[2]

Mass illiteracy, poverty and repressive press laws were serious handicaps to the development of the Indian press. Yet the availability and expansion of printing technology to Indian languages radically changed the face of journalism. Within a century of the publication of the *Bengal Gazette*, there were more than 140 newspapers in Indian languages, articulating a nascent nationalism.

The influence of the Indian language newspapers had grown so much by 1870s that they were perceived as a threat by the colonial administrations, which led to the Vernacular Press Act of 1878, aimed at silencing any attempts by the Indian language press to criticise the government.

As nationalism evolved, so did the idea that the freedom of the press was one of the basic democratic rights to be cherished and fought for. Indian industrialists started their own newspapers with clear anti-colonial stances. Most nationalist leaders were involved in activist, campaigning journalism, none more than Mahatma Gandhi, who realised the importance of the written word and used Gujarati, his mother-tongue, as well as English, to spread the message of freedom. Writing in *Young India* in 1920, he defended the right of the press to protest against press laws: "The stoppage of the circulation of potent ideas that may destroy the Government or compel repentance will be the least among the weapons in its armoury. We must therefore devise methods of circulating our ideas unless and until the whole Press becomes fearless, defies consequences and publishes ideas, even when it is in disagreement with them, just for the purpose of securing its freedom" (Gandhi, 1970: 59).

By 1941, about 4,000 newspapers and magazines were in print in 17 languages and the underlying theme was the end of colonial rule, although they were also used by various sections of the nationalist movement to promote their own political agendas.[3]

The Media at Independence

The violent legacy of Partition dictated that the national media had to be very sensitive to ethnic, cultural and religious considerations. The journalists' task was to help in overcoming the immediate crisis of political instability that followed independence and to foster the long-term process of modernisation and nation-building, reflecting the dominant ideology of the newly emergent and activist state. In addition, the integration of 500 princely states into one nation necessitated that the radio, the only medium of mass appeal at the time, had to be used to develop "national consciousness". In a vast, geographically and culturally diverse country, with 16 official languages and more than 800 dialects and great disparity in the levels of development among the regions and the people, a national media had a crucial role to play in developing a sense of Indianness.

Even after independence, the legacy of anti-colonialism continued to influence the Indian press. India inherited from the British the combination of a private press and a government-controlled broadcasting system. Given the diversity of the press, it showed critical awareness and, by and large, acted as a fourth estate in a fledgling democracy, while the electronic media was used for what came to be known as "nation-building".

All India Radio (AIR), *Aakaashvani*, was seen as a crucial instrument for national development in a hugely illiterate country and the leadership was keen to develop this as a means of mass persuasion[4] but as leaders

elsewhere in the developing world, Indian leaders found it difficult to re-
linquish political control over broadcasting. The political establishment
tried to justify this in terms of the need to use its radio for "development"
purposes. It was also argued that an uncontrolled broadcasting system
could destabilise the country, given its traumatic birth which saw one
million people killed and more than 15 million displaced as the result of
Partition, as the British divided and quit India in 1947.

A year later, India's first prime minister, Jawaharlal Nehru, told the Con-
stituent Assembly which was drafting India's constitution, "my own view
of the set up for broadcasting is that we should approximate as far as possible to the British model, the BBC; that is to say, it would be better if we
had a semi-autonomous corporation. Now I think that is not immediately
feasible" (quoted in Chatterjee, 1991: 182). Consequently, the public
broadcasting monopoly became little more than a propaganda service for
the government. Like other public-sector departments it was over-
bureaucratised and its performance was dull. How far it succeeded in serving any developmental purposes is also open to debate.

The introduction of television in 1959 as a pilot UNESCO-sponsored
educational project reflected the initial attitude to the medium as an educational tool and a means for disseminating state policies and public information. The state television channel (Doordarshan) formed part of AIR until
1976 when it became a separate department under the Information and
Broadcasting Ministry. The aim of the national broadcasters was to educate,
inform and create a feeling of national identity and help maintain national
unity. Doordarshan followed the AIR broadcasting code which prohibited,
among other things, criticism of friendly countries, attack on religions or
communities, incitement to violence or material affecting the integrity of
the nation.[5]

Other sections of the electronic media were also employed by the state
for propaganda purposes. Newsreels produced by the Indian Film Division, a wing of the Ministry of Information and Broadcasting, were used
to promote government policies. As a study by the Press Institute of India
observed, newsreels "are not only controlled by the government but their
theme and content are also dictated by it. Since films have a tremendous
educational and propaganda value, it is mandatory for all cinema houses
to show newsreels..." (Bhattacharjee, 1972: 21)

In addition, the government could indirectly influence the private print
media, through control of newsprint and advertising and subsidising pro-
government newspapers and news agencies. Given the sheer linguistic
and cultural diversity of India, government support was necessary, espe-

cially in the case of regional and small-scale newspapers and magazines. The government therefore subsidised the national news agencies – *Press Trust of India* and *United News of India* in English; and *Smachar Bharati* and *Hindustan Samachar* to cater to regional languages. These agencies were a lifeline for newspapers across the country. As one commentator put it: "Whatever the weaknesses and failings, the Indian news agencies are extraordinary performers in the developing world: without their solid and unfailing service over the decades, the Indian press could not have possibly retained its diversity and pluralism, and small and medium newspapers could not have survived or come up in various Indian languages" (Ram, 1994: 2790).

It is also beyond dispute that the relative autonomy of the print media contributed greatly to the evolution of democracy in India. As democracy took root, various political parties and groupings – representing the whole range of the ideological spectrum – started up their own newspapers and newsletters. Even among the mainstream press, ideological leanings, reflecting political and cultural affiliations, could be detected in the tone, tenor and treatment of stories. More importantly, the pro-active and investigative, often adversarial, role of journalists contributed to the evolution of an early-warning system for serious food shortage and thus a preventive mechanism against famine – an annual scourge during the British Raj (Ram, 1990).

During Nehru's Prime Ministership (1947-1964), the Indian media seemed to follow the democratic agenda set by the government. Most newspapers, even the ones owing allegiance to extreme political parties, believed that a multi-party system of government had taken a firm root in the country and that a free press was integral to its success. Unlike most other developing countries, the government in India accepted criticism and promoted open debate in the editorial pages of national newspapers. This tolerance gave Indian journalists – most coming from an urban middle class milieu – high professional standards and a space in which to engage in critical debates on socio-political and economic issues. Nehru, himself a distinguished writer, had a genuine interest in promoting national consensus through the mass media. His intellectual stature and charisma as the undisputed leader of the Congress party, and indeed the country, further strengthened his position. However, the political manipulations which became the hallmark of Nehru's daughter Indira Gandhi, Prime Minister from 1967 to 1977 and again from 1980 to 1984, strained this national consensus.

Indeed, the close relationship between the media elite and the political establishment broke down completely during the Emergency of 1975-77 when censorship was rife, journalists were detained, the electricity supply

cut off to opposition newspapers, notably the right-wing *Indian Express*
and the centrist *The Statesman*, and national broadcasting organisations
were reduced to becoming the mouthpiece of the ruling congress party
and its leader Indira Gandhi. During this period critics called the AIR the "All
Indira Radio".

Realising the effectiveness of the media image and convinced that television can be used to retain power, Indira Ghandi decided in 1976 to
delink Doordarshan from AIR and make it a separate department of the
Information and Broadcasting ministry. Despite blatant appropriation of
the electronic media, she lost the 1977 election to the Janata Party – a loose
grouping of right-wing and centrist parties supported by the communists.
The fact that for the first time a non-Congress coalition had taken power
in New Delhi had a positive impact on the growth of Indian media, partly
because it catapulted several regional leaders into the national limelight,
thereby promoting the regional press; and partly because it was a reaction
to the muzzling of the press during the Emergency.

The Janata government promised autonomy for the electronic media
and appointed a 12-member working group (known as Verghese Committee under the chairmanship of journalist B. G. Verghese) to suggest
policy formulations for the broadcast media. The result of their delibera-
tions published in 1978 – the *Prasar Bharati Bill*, as it was called – recom-
mended the establishment of an independent National Broadcasting Trust,
named *Akash Bharati,* to run both Doordarshan and AIR.[6]

However, aware that control of the airwaves was crucial in a largely
illiterate country, the Janata government introduced a much diluted *Akash
Bharati Bill* in parliament, ignoring the key recommendation that the new
broadcasting organisation should be independent of the government. It
was not until 1980, when Gandhi returned to power, that the Bill was placed
before Parliament and voted down. But in 1982 she set up a working group,
chaired by the economist P. C. Joshi, with the narrowly defined mandate
to evaluate and make suggestions for programming on Doordarshan. It
took a year for the Joshi Committee to complete its report and another 18
months for the government to present it to Parliament. The committee
sought to introduce a significant public service component in Doordarshan's
output, with its emphasis on developmental coverage and making sure that
the country's diversity was represented in its programming.[7]

Colour was introduced in 1982 in time for the live coverage of the Asian
Games which Indira Gandhi saw as a showcase for the achievements of
Indian broadcasting. She also gave high priority to the launching of
INSAT1 (Indian National Satellite) and the rapid increase in the number

of transmitters from 14 in 1977 to 175 in 1985, with television signals reaching 392 million in 1985. As Manjunath Pendakur argues, this spree was intended in part "simply to spread the magic and myth of the ruling family" (Pendakur, 1991: 248).

As Doordarshan extended its reach and hours of programming it required more material to fill the schedule. To meet this need it looked to the burgeoning Hindi film industry and in 1982 started showing Hindi films weekly. The first soap opera *Hum Log*, telecast in 1984, dealt with contemporary social problems and ran for 156 episodes. Then came the extraordinarily popular Hindu epics *Ramayana* (1987) and *Mahabharata* (1988-89).[8]

Doordarshan became increasingly commercialised during the 1980s. This process had already begun in 1976 with selling of airtime for advertising and commercial sponsorship for programmes from 1980. This commercialisation was intensified by the increasingly neo-liberal governments of the 1980s. As a result, television became much more entertainment oriented; its soaps were altered to meet the needs of advertisers. As Rajagopal (1993: 103-104) argues: "The family planning theme was diluted, family harmony was stressed instead, and the plot was speeded up" as prime time became entertainment-based. As a result, Doordarshan began to draw large audiences and its advertising revenues rose substantially.

Like other aspects of Indian industries, the media sector was also fundamentally transformed by the liberalisation of the Indian economy introduced in 1991 by the government of P. V. Narasimha Rao, as India was forced to open up its economy to Western capital in the wake of the disintegration of the Soviet Union, with which India had maintained close economic and security ties during the Cold War era.

Rao's Congress government announced a new economic policy that began the process of privatisation, dismantling the "licence-quota-permit raj" and throwing the economy open to international capital, under the influence of the Structural Adjustment Programme imposed by the World Bank and the International Monetary Fund. Under this new dispensation, the government ordered Doordarshan to generate its own revenues for further expansion, forcing it to become a commercial television service, although the public service remit continued to be considered important.

The Satellite Invasion

Like television, satellites too were introduced into Indian broadcasting as part of a developmental project to overcome the technical problems of terrestrial broadcasting over such huge geographical areas.[9]

One key consequence of the opening up of the economy was the entry of foreign, mainly Western, commercial satellite television in what used to be one of the most closed broadcasting systems in any democracy. The first major event to be shown via these satellites was the live coverage of the 1990 Gulf crisis by the Atlanta-based Cable News Network (CNN), which found a ready audience among the Indian metropolitan elite. This was followed in 1991 by a five-channel satellite service (Plus, Prime Sports, Channel V [an Indianised imitation of MTV], the BBC World, and Movie, India's first pay channel) by Hong Kong based STAR TV (Satellite Television Asian Region), eventually controlled by Australian-born US multimedia mogul Rupert Murdoch.[10]

The satellite channels, not bound by the public service codes and conventions, became an instant hit with Indian middle classes because of their lively approach to programming and, more importantly, with advertisers who saw India as an "emerging market" for transnational corporations. By 1997, more than 65 cable and satellite channels were operating in India including big transnational media corporations, notably, Star, BBC, MTV, Sony, CNN, Disney and NBC, and scores of Indian companies.

However, as the private Indian media firms and Doordarshan took on the new challenges from the transnational media companies, the TNCs too had to adjust their strategies to suit the Indian context. Star, for example, felt that since its programming was in English, it was only reaching a tiny, though influential and wealthy, urban audience. So it started providing Hindi sub-titles to Hollywood films, broadcast on its 24-hour channel Star Movies. In 1996 it started dubbing popular American soaps like *The Bold and Beautiful* into Hindi and showing exclusive entertainment programmes, including movies in Hindi. BBC World, too, realised the benefits of going local and broadcast "India specific" programmes about the country or on topics that would interest the Indian market. (*The Economic Times Brand Equity* – 20-26 August 1997).

The most successful of these enterprises was Zee TV, the first Hindi satellite channel in India, launched in October 1992. This Indian owned private network which claimed to be a family entertainment channel, thrived on a mixture of Hindi film and film-based programming, serials, music countdowns and quiz contests. Zee's innovative programming, including the news, in 'Hinglish' (a mixture of Hindi and English) became extremely popular with its growing audience – today, it reaches approximately 120 million homes.[11] Zee set the standard for private television in India. Its flexible advertising breaks, and its practice of putting sponsors' names on programmes made it popular among advertisers and it broke even within the first six months of its launch. In 1993, Murdoch became a 49.9 per cent partner with Zee TV. Since then the Zee group has launched EL Television in 1995, showing movies and music and Zee Cinema in 1996, a pay channel.

Among the regional channels, the most successful was Sun TV, the first Tamil language satellite channel, launched in 1993. SUN Music and SUN Movies were added a year later. AsiaNet, the first regional language cable network, which has now become a household name in the southern state of Kerala, was another success story. Just four years after its launch in 1993, the channel was reaching 10 million viewers, including one million in the Gulf countries, home to millions of Keralite immigrants. (*The Asian Age,* 14 July 1997).

The impact on Doordarshan

The satellite channels revolutionised Indian broadcasting. Their entertainment programmes were slickly produced and marketed and the news and current affairs programming was less biased than Doordarshan's. The private channels acted as a catalyst to the drab and dull public service broadcaster, putting an end to its monopoly and forcing it to add new channels and introduce a gradual glasnost in news and analysis. They intensified the state broadcaster's efforts to hold onto audience shares and advertising revenues, although the Doordarshan network in 1992 had an audience of 195 million home viewers. In 1993 five new Doordarshan satellite channels were introduced – Metro (an entertainment channel aimed at the younger generation), Business, Music, Sports and Infotainment (films, news, wildlife and travel programmes).

The growth of satellite/cable services and video sales to diasporic communities was also seen as a potential market opportunity. In March 1995 the international channel of Doordarshan was launched, reaching 50 countries. A month later, a 24 hour movie channel, showing films in Hindi, English and regional languages was started. In 1997, Doordarshan had three national channels, two special interest channels, ten regional channels and an international channel. DDI, a terrestrial service with national, regional, local and educational productions, is the channel with the widest geographical reach in India, available to 86 per cent of the population. Doordarshan has also entered into tie-ups with CNN and with MTV to provide programming (McDowell, 1997: 167). Moreover, to deal with challenges from regional satellite channels such as Sun TV, Doordarshan developed the Regional Language Satellite Service which has separate channels allocated for major languages.

Impact on the Press

While globalisation has revolutionised Indian television it is also having an impact on the traditionally left-of-centre-leaning mainstream press, influenced in no small measure by Nehruvian socialism, the staple ideological diet of independent India.

As Western media conglomerates mount pressure to expand their operations in India, there has been unease in some quarters of the media as they weigh up the implications of foreign ownership of the Indian press. Among the main bidders are the London *Financial Times*, which plans to team up with *Business Standard* of Calcutta to start a new business daily, and *Time* magazine, keen to produce an Indian edition in collaboration with the Living Media group, publishers of *India Today*, which has already launched an Indian edition of *Cosmopolitan* magazine.[12]

Unlike many developing countries, most newspapers in India are run by Indians who fear a loss of identity if the foreign media are allowed majority ownership. Given the power of US-dominated Western media, there is concern that competition could drive Indian national newspapers out of the market, or at least reduce the rich diversity of a press that represents a multiplicity of interests and political opinions – New Delhi alone has more than a dozen daily newspapers.

Nevertheless, the serious and staid Indian press is already copying US-style sensational journalism. Journalistic practice and training, already much influenced by Western journalism, is being further Americanised, with greater emphasis on entertainment-oriented news agendas. The increasingly vicious circulation wars and the managerial approach to running editorial operations, most acutely seen in the venerated *Times of India*, are symptoms of how globalisation is affecting even the most traditional of Indian newspapers.[13] *The Times*, wrote one observer, "is no longer the newspaper for the most authoritative reports on government and politics, [...] The most successful circulation-booster has been a weekly colour magazine insert called E-Times, full of gossip about film stars and the coming week's cable-TV programming. Markets follow the market" (McDonald, 1995: 25).

However, while the English-language elite publications are experiencing a declining circulation and a dilution of content, the newspapers and magazines in Indian languages have witnessed a renaissance. Media globalisation has hit India at a time when the country has witnessed an extraordinary growth of vernacular newspapers and regional language television channels. The changing contours of national politics, with regional parties taking centre-stage, has given a new impetus to newspapers in Indian languages. The development and spread of personal computers and the offset press have revolutionised the newspaper industry. According to the latest figures from the Indian Newspaper Society, publications in Indian languages sold four times more than English language publications.[14]

Analysing the data from the Annual Report of the Registrar for Newspapers, Robin Jeffrey comments: "In 1961, circulation of Hindi dailies by the most generous estimate was 750,000 copies: English 1.3 million – in effect 1.7 English dailies for every one in Hindi. By 1992, Hindi dailies claimed sales of 11.2 million to 3.9 million for English – a ratio of 2.9 Hindi dailies for each one in English" (Jeffrey, 1997:78).

As regional parties gain ascendancy in Indian politics and literacy expands to rural communities, newspapers in Indian languages are likely to show further growth. This raises the question of how the regionalisation/localisation of the media will affect the press's role as articulating a sense of national identity, which at the same time is being threatened by globalisation. However, in compensation, this role may be taken over by a growing national audience for television, which is not dependent on literacy. It could also be argued that the vigour of a regional press will promote and feed into a more dynamic and representative national media system.

Indian Media, Global Challenge

The growing commercialisation of the national broadcaster and the increasing commodification of news and information have undermined the original social objectives of the media. The growing popularity of private television has made Doordarshan's aim of informing the masses difficult since it now has the dual task of educating as well as providing mass entertainment to remain competitive.

Given the reach of the terrestrial broadcasting network – it now covers nearly 450 million people in 86 per cent of the country – the government (a 13-party coalition led by Inder Kumar Gujral) has been supportive of Doordarshan, for example by refusing permission for the uplinking of satellite companies in India. Even Indian companies, such as Zee, have to uplink in Hong Kong. The government also gives it access denied to the foreign media. For example, during the 50th anniversary of India's Independence celebrations on August 15, 1997, only Doordarshan was allowed to telecast live the special midnight session of Parliament. The ban imposed on Direct to Home (DTH) reception is another measure that the government has taken to safeguard the official media, although Jaipal

Reddy, Information and Broadcasting Minister, says that the ban is temporary and once the rules have been laid down under the Broadcast Bill, DTH will be allowed through bidding. (*The Pioneer,* August 18, 1997).[15]

The Broadcast Bill, introduced in May 1997, seeks to bring order to the broadcasting industry, currently regulated by the archaic Telegraph Act of 1885. The bill seeks to create an independent Broadcasting Authority "for the purpose of promoting, facilitating and regulating broadcasting services in India." Private channels have to apply to this authority for a licence. Doordarshan is exempt since it is a public broadcaster, so are sports and international news channels such as BBC and CNN.

The bill divides broadcast services into six categories – terrestrial radio, satellite radio, terrestrial TV channels, satellite TV channels, DTH broadcasters and local delivery services. An operator can get a licence for only one category. Foreign nationals, allowed up to 49 per cent on foreign equity in satellite channels, cannot invest in terrestrial networks. This is obviously not liked by transnational media companies, as one of their key representatives in India argued: "It is impractical for transnational broadcasters to get into join ventures with varying equity structures in each country where their signals are downlinked"[16] (*India Today,* June 30, 1997).

The bill also seeks to introduce cross-media ownership restrictions, with print media owners not allowed to hold more than a 20 per cent stake in a TV channel. This aspect of the bill has generated much criticism from the top media houses in India. The comment of *India Today* is typical of the sentiment: "The bill will hinder the growth of consumers' choice by keeping the Government too much in the picture, and by introducing a licence-permit raj in the sky" (*India Today,* March 15, 1997).

Several people in India, including the Press Council Chairman, Justice P. B. Sawant, want the bill to be scrapped and the 1990 *Prasar Bharati* (Broadcasting Corporation of India) Act, which gives autonomy to Doordarshan, implemented instead. Further changes in the structure of the public sector broadcasting are likely as Doordarshan gains relative autonomy with the implementation of the *Prasar Bharati* Act which came into force on September 15, 1997. The Act, passed by the Parliament in 1990 but notified for implementation by the government only in July 1997, aims to grant autonomy to Doordarshan and AIR, which will be regulated by *Prasar Bharati*. "The intention is that the proposed corporation should function as a genuinely autonomous body – innovative, dynamic and flexible – with a high degree of credibility."[17]

Despite scepticism from critics who feel that the corporation will be too heavily weighed in favour of the government, the Act is the first step towards autonomy for public service broadcasting, as India grapples with the challenges and opportunities offered by globalisation. Though Doordarshan's reach has been extended and new channels added, the percentage of public service programmes has decreased, as it begins to respond to increasing commercial pressures. For survival, it has to become more competitive in the entertainment and information field as the foreign media companies are fast adapting to India's enormous needs in these areas.[18]

A public-service broadcaster and a committed and independent press can play an important role in educating and informing the Indian people. Even after 50 years of independence nearly half of the population is still illiterate and 60% live below the poverty line. Therefore the need for public-service broadcasting and educational journalism remains particularly acute.

At the same time there is a great potential for commercial television in India and overseas, especially through the export of Indian programming as a result of the digital revolution. Already, Zee TV is available to the Indian diaspora in Britain, TV Asia in North America and AsiaNet in the Gulf region. The Doordarshan International is to be turned into a round-the-clock channel. It is also planning to start an exclusive news and current affairs channel (*Cable Waves,* June 16-30, 1997). Doordarshan may emerge as the major partner with international broadcasters that wish to gain access to Indian audiences or to obtain live coverage of Indian issues, as with the Doordarshan-CNN tie up (McDowell, 1997:169).

As output from a reinvigorated Indian television and newspapers becomes available outside the country, India, given its competence in English, the language of the international media, could become the first Third World nation to make a significant presence on the US-dominated global media market.[19] As Jacka and Ray argue: "The global reach of Indian television can only be expected to increase in the coming years. As free-to-air or ordinary broadcast television reaches its finite limits, expatriate Indians (usually wealthy) will become a crucial source of revenue" (Jacka and Ray, 1996: 98-99).

Globalisation has provided Indian talent with an opportunity to expand beyond the borders of India. As the electronic media becomes more open, the kinds of debates and discussions which have given vitality to the print media in India will also liven up small screens in India and among the Indian diaspora.

Despite claims of "cultural imperialism" and a loss of identity under the avalanche of Western television images, it is instructive to note that the most successful private television channel – Zee TV – is making programmes, on Indian themes, in Hindi. The growth of private channels in regional languages and the extraordinary development of the language press in India – the largest selling newspaper in India continues to be *Malayala Manorama*, a regional newspaper – is a testimony to the cultural strengths of India. These are reassuring thoughts on the 50th anniversary of India's independence.

NOTES

1. It was started by James Augustus Hicky a disgruntled employee of the East India Company who described the journal as "A weekly political and commercial paper open to all parties, but influenced by none", quoted in Rau, 1974: 10.
2. For a discussion on the role the press played in developing nationalist consciousness, see Desai, 1976: 221-239.
3. During the closing days of the British administration, the press could be broadly divided into three categories: the establishment papers such as *The Statesman* and the *Times of India*; the nationalist press including *Hindustan Times*, *The Indian Express* and *The Hindu*; and among the key Indian language publications: *Anand Bazaar Patrika* in Bengali, *Kesari* in Marathi, *Sandesh* and *Bombay Samachar* in Gujarati, *Matribhumi* in Malayalam and *Aaj* in Hindi.
4. The first radio programme was broadcast in 1923 but AIR's regular broadcasting service began in 1927 and was founded as a public broadcasting service in 1936. At independence it had only six stations to cover a vast country like India, but by 1996 there were 185 broadcasting centres, including 72 local radio stations, covering more than 97 per cent of the country's population. At the time of independence there were an estimated 275,000 receiving sets; in 1996 there were 111 million. AIR is among the largest radio networks in the world and produces programmes in 24 languages and 146 dialects (All India Radio, 1996: 17).
5. Among the social objectives of Doordarshan were: to promote national integration, to act as a catalyst for social change, to create values of appraisal of art and cultural heritage, to highlight the need for social welfare including the welfare of women, children and the less privileged

and to provide essential information to stimulate agricultural development and to disseminate the message of family planning.

6. In 1964, when Indira Gandhi was the Information and Broadcasting minister, there was an attempt to make AIR a BBC style corporation and a committee under the chairmanship of A. K. Chanda (a former auditor general of India) studied how this could be done. Two years later, when the committee submitted its recommendations – which included that television be separated from AIR and given a 20 year developmental plan and that broadcasting be structured along the lines of the BBC – they were ignored by the government.

7. A New Delhi journal, *Mainstream*, published volume 2 of the Report which contains the summary of observations and recommendations. 'An Indian Personality for Television - Report of the Working Group on Software for Doordarshan', *Mainstream*, April 14, 1984, pp. 27-33 April 21, 1984, pp. 16-23 & April 28, 1984, pp. 14-23, May 5, 1984. pp. 14-19.

8. Borrowing from the success of telenovelas, in Brazil and Mexico, the Indian government started using education entertainers – a mix of education, information and entertainment. Other serials aired at Doordarshan with a strong social and cultural component were *Chanakya*, based on the life of an ancient Indian economist and philosopher, and *Saurabhi*, which draws on the rich cultural diversity of India. Doordarshan also tended to produce and circulate a "Hindu-Hindi" image of Indian national identity. As Mitra puts it: "In some ways, television has drawn heavily from cinema, and somewhat from traditional mass media. It has also re-coded the literary texts, from various languages, constantly trying to create a cultural ensemble that will overcome the diversity of cultural practices that are found in India. Yet in doing this, it has often remained Hindi- and Delhi-centric" (Mitra 1990:174).

9. It was not CNN, though, that brought satellite into India for the first time but SITE (Satellite Instructional Television Experiment) launched in 1975 to expand the reach of the social educational programmes of Doordarshan to remote village. See Agrawal, 1981: 136-146.

10. For a good discussion of how STAR TV was received in Asia see Chan 1994: 112-31. Other transnational media corporations active in India include: NBC, which came in 1996, aimed at the business community and is planning to go into Hindi programming with film-based shows. Sony Entertainment Television, available since 1995, shows

English programmes dubbed in Hindi and Hindi movies. ESPN, the 24 hour sports channel, was launched in India in 1995; Time Warner with its Cartoon Network and TNT, the movie channel.

11. Zee TV is the leader in satellite television in India. Seventy per cent of the advertising revenue from television goes to Doordarshan, whose reach extends to 67% of the Indian television territory as satellite is not yet available to them. Half of the remaining 30% in one third of the country, which is shared by the more than 65 satellite and cable channels, goes to Zee TV and its two other channels. The remaining 15% is shared by all the other channels.

12. *India Today*, the largest circulated English news magazine in the country, which also has editions in five Indian languages – Hindi, Telugu, Gujarati, Malayalam and Tamil – is the most widely read publication in India with a circulation of 1.2 million copies and an estimated readership of 11.4 million (*India Today*, June 9, 1997).

13. According to one account, Samir Jain the chief executive of *The Times of India* is "credited with 'Americanising' *The Times of India*, and imposing Harvard Business School techniques that he picked up during a short internship at *The New York Times*." For an interesting account of how he runs his newspaper empire see Coleridge, 1993: 220-241.

14. According to the Indian Newspaper Society, in 1996 there were 70 dailies, 26 weeklies, 23 fortnightlies, 56 monthlies and two others accounting for 177 publications in the English language alone. The entire English language press accounted for a circulation of a mere 9.3 million, nearly half of this was for daily newspaper sales. The growth is much more robust in the Indian languages. In 1996, there were 324 dailies, 79 weeklies, 33 fortnightlies, 96 monthlies and 7 others, totalling 539. They had nearly four times the circulation figures of the English publications at more than 37 million, with more than half of this circulation – 19.6 million – accounted for by dailies. (*Business India*, March 24-April 6 1997)

15. Leader of the private channels lobbying to launch DTH is Star TV, which has reportedly invested $8 million to provide 40 channels through ISkyB (India Sky Broadcasting), set up by Murdoch.

16. Rathikant Basu, a former Director General of Doordarshan, who became CEO of Star TV in 1996, was indicted by a parliamentary accounts committee for allegedly giving assent to a "friendly deal" with a private TV company that caused Rs 3.52 crore (approx. $1 million) revenue loss to the government (*The Asian Age*, 23 August 1997).

17. Statement of Objectives and Reasons, *Prasar Bharati Broadcasting Corporation of India Bill* 1989, Government of India, New Delhi.

18. Despite exaggerated claims about the popularity of Western-owned or inclined channels, Doordarshan continues to receive most viewers. According to the weekly surveys conducted by the Indian Market Research Bureau, the state broadcaster continues to enjoy much higher ratings compared to those of the private channels. "Since foreign channels find a lot of space in English newspapers, there is a perception in the urban areas that they enjoy a large viewership. But the ground reality is entirely different," says Dr B. S. Chandrasekhar, head of Doordarshan's audience research unit (*The Asian Age,* 14 July 1997).

19. Already, Indian publications such as *India Abroad, Asian Age,* and *India Today* can be found on news-stands in many parts of the globe. *Economic and Political Weekly* – one of the most intellectually demanding publications anywhere – is available on campuses worldwide.

REFERENCES

Agrawal, B. C., "Anthropological applications in communication research and evaluation of SITE in India", *Media Asia*, Vol. 8. No. 3, 1981:136-146.

Bhattacharjee, A., *The Indian Press – Profession to Industry*, New Delhi: Vikas, 1972.

"Message for the media", *Business India,* March 24-April 6 1997: 54-60.

Chan, J. M., "National responses and accessibility to STAR TV in Asia", *Journal of Communication*, Vol. 44, No. 3, 1994:112-31.

Chatterjee, P. C., *Broadcasting in India*, New Delhi: Sage, 1991.

Coleridge, N., *Paper Tigers*, London: Heinemann, 1993.

Desai, A. R., *Social Background of Indian Nationalism*, 5th edition, Bombay: Popular, 1976.

Gandhi, M. K., *Gandhi – Essential Writings*, edited by V. V. Ramana Murti, New Delhi: Gandhi Peace Foundation, 1970.

Jacka E. & Ray, M., "Indian Television: An Emerging Regional Force" in Sinclair, J. Jacka E and Cunningham, S. (eds.), *New Patterns in Global Television – Peripheral Vision*, Oxford: Oxford University Press, 1996.

Jeffrey, R., "Hindi: 'Taking to the *Punjab Kesari* Line'", "*Economic and Political Weekly,* January 18 1997:77-83.

McDonald, H., "Paper Tigers", *Far Eastern Economic Review,* October 5, 1995:24-30.

McDowell, S., "Globalization and policy choices: television and audio-visual services policies in India", *Media, Culture and Society*, Vol. 19, 1997:151-172.

Mitra, A., "The Position of Television in the Cultural Map of India", *Media Asia*, Vol. 17, No. 3, 1990:166-76.

Pendakur, M., "Political Economy of Television in India" in Sussman, G. and Lent, J. (eds.), *Transnational Communications: Wiring the Third World*, London: Sage, 1991.

Rajagopal, A., "The rise of national programming: the case of Indian television", *Media, Culture and Society*, Vol. 15, 1993:91-111.

Ram, N. "An Independent Press and Anti-Hunger Strategies: The Indian Experience" in Dreze, J. and Sen, A. (eds.) The *Political Economy of Hunger*, Vol. I, Oxford: Clarendon Press, 1990.

Ram, N. "Foreign Media Entry into the Press - Issues and Implications", *Economic and Political Weekly*, October 22, 1994: 2787-2790.

Rau, M. C., *The Press*, New Delhi: National Book Trust, 1974.

Government Reports

Ministry of Information and Broadcasting, Annual Report 1996-97
All India Radio 1996
Prasar Bharati Broadcasting Corporation of India Bill 1989

Newspapers and Magazines

The Pioneer
Cable Waves
The Economic Times
The Asian Age
India Today

INDIA ON THE SCREEN IN THE 1980s AND 1990s

SARA MARTÍN ALEGRE
Universitat Autònoma de Barcelona

According to Sumita Chakravarty, "since 1971, India has been leading the world in film production" (1993: 9). Over the 1980s, Indian film factories have produced an average 800 films a year, which is an extraordinary figure compared to the 450 produced in the USA or the 500 produced in Europe every year. Yet, the India that the West has seen on its screens is not the one of the many Indian films, but the India of a few British and American films. This situation has not changed much in the last fifteen years, the period this paper roughly covers. In comparison to the status achieved by the literature written in English by Indian writers, both living in India and abroad, Indian cinema is far behind as concerns its presence in the cultural life of the West. On the other hand, the India portrayed by 1980s and 1990s films made by Western film makers seems to lag also far behind the representations of India in contemporary literature, and tends to perpetuate a sentimental, romanticised portrait of India that is blatantly colonialist while pretending not to be so.

The electronic postmodern world is in fact rather limited when it comes to the circulation of films not only between the East and the West but also within the West itself. As Edward Said noted in *Orientalism,* "[t]elevision, the films, and all the media's resources have forced information into more and more standardized molds"; he further argues that "standardization and cultural stereotyping have intensified the hold of the nineteenth-century academic and imaginative demonology of 'the mysterious Orient' " (1985: 26). In the case of India, the romantic image derived from the nineteenth-century imperial rhetoric – which is the one basically kept in film – coexists with a newer India of the media, presented as a land of natural and man-made catastrophes, and extreme poverty. However, the point Said misses is that the contemporary cultural standardisation of national iden-

tities by the electronic world goes much beyond Orientalism and territorial imperialism. Furthermore, it is a process that affects not only the ex-
colonial territories but all the nations of the world, possibly including the
USA itself, where most of these misrepresentations originate. Orientalism
is ironically turning to have its questionable compensations. It is because
of the work of people such as Said that it was felt in the 1980s that a new
direction should be taken in the representation of India on film. The image of Hollywood India was perceived to be wrong, and there was an interest in altering it, beginning with Richard Attenborough's *Gandhi* (1982).
One can easily think of four remarkable Western films about India made
in the last fifteen years: *Gandhi* itself, James Ivory's *Heat and Dust* (1983),
David Lean's *A Passage to India* (1985), and Roland Joffe's *City of Joy* (1992).
Biased as these films may be, it is hard to think of any other foreign nation
that has attracted the attention of the West to such an extent, to the point
that it must be claimed that India has, in fact, a privileged presence on the
screens of the West.

It may be argued that such attention does not benefit India and that it
actually perpetuates cultural stereotypes while preventing Indian films
from reaching Western screens. Representations of foreign cultures are
necessarily misrepresentations, but at the same time they are an indication of an interest that we should be sorry to give up in favour of being just
passive receivers of the self-representations other nations have to offer.
Edward Said argues in *Culture and Imperialism* that "all cultures tend to make
representations of foreign cultures the better to master or in some way
control them. Yet not all cultures make representations of foreign cultures
and in fact master or control them. This is the distinction, I believe, of
modern Western cultures" (1993: 100). It seems to me that here Said is
being both unfair and inaccurate. For one thing, international cultural
relations are not all based on a rhetoric of control and submission; there is
a cultural space beyond colonialism in which some nations will offer sympathetic representations of foreign nations they feel close to or interested
in, rather than attempt to dominate them. On the other hand, Said himself falls here into the trap of misrepresenting the West as a monolithic
entity implacably using representation to colonise other cultures, ignoring thus the differences between the nations of the West and the fact that
not all relate in an imperialistic, colonialist way to other nations. Furthermore, Said argues that the representation of foreign cultures is the first
step towards controlling them, but, in fact, the USA has invented a new
mode of colonisation in which not even the more or less biased knowl-

edge of the colonised matters – actually, the colonised are the ones who must bother to learn the nuances of the national identity imposed on them. Hollywood executives do not think of Finland, Portugal, Japan or India as nationalities to be conquered through representations but as markets where they can sell products that represent America. That is to say, despite how little British people learned about Indian identity, they were forced to know at least enough to colonise the country, whereas the USA may totally ignore the reality of, for instance, Spain, yet still colonise the Spanish film screens. What is more, India may answer back to Britain and reject the image imposed on it, as many Indian writers are doing now – but, does it make sense for Spain, or for that matter, for all of Europe, to answer back to Hollywood? Would the USA notice?

Sumita Chakravarty explains that Indian films are a "product of British colonialism" (*op. cit.,* 133) and that because of this, Indian films are "nurtured in a chronic state of underdevelopment". She argues that the growth of Indian cinema "has been haphazard and subject to random and, in general, repressive legislation (very high rates of taxation, strict and unimaginative censorship)". Despite this, the three main Indian centres of production, Bombay, Calcutta and Madras, have kept up a steady flow of production. Why, then, haven't Indian films flooded the screens of the West since the West seems to be interested in India? Apart from the obvious problem that the distribution of films abroad is very expensive and constricted by American distributors, there are other factors. One of them is the status of film in India itself. This is epitomised by the tragic fate of uncle Hanif in Rushdie's *Midnight Children*. Hanif wants to make realistic films about the 'real' India, but, his wife – a famous actress who has starred in countless song and dance films – rightly argues that Indian filmgoers, who are mainly working class, do not want to see real India on the screen, but the India of the popular Bombay film; this is the world they want to escape into for very good, respectable reasons. Like Hanif, many Indians have felt this is not the kind of film India should make, yet Hanif's suicide may indicate that rejecting Indian popular culture is a dead-end for Indian film making.

Realistic films go against the grain in India, as the concept, Chakravarty argues, is "alien to Indian philosophic and aesthetic traditions" (*ibid.,* 85). For her, realistic Indian films are translations of a frame provided by the West and deny a tradition that is closer to the Indian artistic traditions, that of the Bombay popular film. Furthermore, Chakravarty notes that "the call for realism meant that the cinema should project not images of what Indian society was but what it *should be*... Realism is the masquerading moral conscience of the Indian intelligentsia in their assumed (though not uncontested) role of national leadership" (ibid., 85), especially reinforced during the 1950s when Indian films started being presented abroad. This same intelligentsia "labelled the commercial cinema an impersonating, debased, and parasitic form, thereby seeking to maintain and police cultural boundaries" (*ibid.*, 5). Meanwhile, Indian popular cinema was creating a more authentic, national identity, without referents in the cinema of the West, which is why she concludes that "the popular cinema has been deeply implicated, if marginalised, in the project of decolonization" (*ibid.*, 15).

We have to understand then, that India has managed to find its own film voice in the Bombay popular film, but that this kind of film is not to be exported precisely because it corresponds to artistic standards very far from those of the West, also adopted by Indian filmmakers working in the realistic tradition. India is not an exception in this, either. Spanish popular films of the 1950s to the 1970s pose the same problem: even though they command very high audience ratings when screened on Spanish TV, they are derided by the intellectuals and the 'serious' filmmakers. These people miss the point that these films are a valid representation of Spanish identity for the many Spaniards who enjoy them. In fact, neither Buñuel nor Almodóvar, the two Spanish filmmakers best known abroad, can be fully understood without a reference to the populism of Spanish films. There is, then, a generalised awareness that the image a nation wants to project abroad may be best defined by its films, but there are also cultural mechanisms operating within the nations that discriminate against popular forms of self-representation in film and that prevent them from being shown abroad, if only as cultural documents.

The Indian government has taken an active part in the promotion of Indian films abroad. The government sponsored the first International festival of India in 1952, an event designed to present Indian films to Western societies. This also began what I would call the hybridisation of Indian films, that is to say, the filming of quality European films, such as Renoir's *The River*, in India. This phenomenon is also comparable to the situation in Scotland, for instance, which is the setting for a number of foreign films, to the point that there is a Scottish Film Location office. Nations that cannot export the products of their local film industry easily often find it convenient to strike this kind of deal. More recently, in the mid-eighties, the government contributed again to raising the standards of Indian film making by sponsoring a number of films which aim at being authentic, realistic representations of India, once more leaving aside the popular film. In the early 1980s, a selection of these new works was presented in a festival held in the USA. Chrakravarty notes that the names of the directors of the Hindi language films screened in this event have become 'passwords' to students of India's new cinema, but it must be remembered that students are not average Western filmgoers and that the impact of these festivals is limited.

Among the Indian hybrid films, the best-known is *Gandhi*, a co-production with Britain shot entirely in India with the collaboration of the National Film Development Corporation. *Gandhi* is addressed both to Indians and non-Indians alike, but seems to be tilted somehow to the tastes of Western consumers. One wonders why, if the financial resources could be mustered, the Indian government itself did not undertake the filming of *Gandhi* on its own. Why let the British define Gandhi's complex figure? Why let the British reap the spate of Oscars the film won? A similar question was asked when Spielberg's *Schindler's List* was released and many Germans lamented having missed the chance to change the image of their own country by publicising the heroic figure of Oskar Schindler. Again, the point is that missed chances have to do with other factors beyond colonialism. Thus, Ridley Scott's reply to the Spanish film critics who disliked his portrait of Christopher Columbus (played by French actor Gerard Depardieu) in his film *1492: The Conquest of Paradise*, was that at least he had bothered to portray Columbus, the Spanish national hero, whereas the Spaniards hadn't; for him, what should be criticised was the short-sightedness of the Spanish producer and not his work. My guess is that precisely the disagreement about the kind of hero Columbus was prevented the making of a high-quality Spanish film about him; Indians may have missed the chance to make *Gandhi*, the film, for similar reasons. Foreigners working with preconceived, stereotypical ideas find it thus easier to fix in static representations issues that are problematic in a dynamic, dialogical way where they originate.

The three other films I am to refer to are all literary adaptations, though of a very different kind. David Lean's *A Passage to India* (1985), which followed in the wake of the success of *Gandhi*, is the adaptation of the respected modern classic by E.M. Forster. *Heat and Dust* (1983) is a product of the Merchant-Ivory factory based on the Ruth Prawer Jabvhala novel awarded the Booker Prize in 1972. She herself wrote the film's screenplay. Finally, Roland Joffe's *City of Joy* (1992) is a free adaptation of Dominique

Lapierre's best-seller, a book that mixes fiction with a considerable amount of factual information about life in Calcutta. These three films bridge the gap between the colonialist and the post-colonialist view of India, though the image of India they offer is bounded by old and new stereotypes. *A Passage to India* presents, like the novel on which it is based, a moment in which the monolithic reality of the British Raj seems to leave room for hope of some form of friendly, free relationship in the future, though this may well be just wishful thinking. No doubt, audiences who saw the film on its release were charmed by Lean's elegant, romanticised portrait of Forster's 1920s India in the same way that Anne, the protagonist of *Heat and Dust*, is charmed by the 1920s India of her distant relative, Olivia, an Englishwoman who dares abandon her British husband for an Indian Nawab. The representation of Anne's 1980s India, a place of squalor which does not live up to its past, is taken up in *City of Joy*. There, what I would call the post-colonial exotic has erased the traces of the romanticised colonial past and what is left is the misery of the Calcutta slums, colonised now for the West's imagination by the late saintly Mother Theresa and the court of amateur European missionaries and would-be heroes this film portrays.

Coming not long after *Gandhi*, both *Heat and Dust* and *A Passage to India* seem to take a step backwards in the way India is represented on the screen. Both look at the odd behaviour of British women in India rather than at the Indians themselves and are, clearly, texts about sexuality in the West rather than portraits of India. Adela Quested, who unfairly accuses Dr. Aziz of having tried to rape her in the Marabar Caves, appears to be the 'heads' of the coin of which Olivia is 'tails'. Adela is momentarily maddened by her inability to cope with the sexuality that Dr. Aziz's presence awakens in her; Olivia lets herself be seduced by the shady Nawab to escape the boredom of married life – British married life, not Indian. As for Anne, she goes even further: Adela remains a virgin, Olivia aborts an Anglo-Indian child nobody wants but Anne has an affair with her Indian landlord – a married man – and, finding she is pregnant, decides to keep her baby without telling him, returning then to England. Anne's secrecy makes her child not the symbol of future reconciliation but yet another example of the grossness of colonial appropriation.

In these two films there is an Indian male protagonist who is the object of the tensions between the British and the Indian communities, but who seems to be in a somewhat isolated position. The rest of Indian characters are either inconspicuous, or strangely silenced – presences but not characters. Thus, in *Heat and Dust*, the Nawab played by Shashi Kapoor is the only English-speaking Indian of the 1920s section of the film. The fact that dialogue in Indian languages is not subtitled in these films leaves the Indian characters, such as the Nawab's mother, stranded in a no man's land; they seem to belong to a closed world totally inaccessible to the West. When conversation takes place, though, as happens in *A Passage to India*, language (always English) seems unable to sustain any real meaning so that only Adela's hysterical reaction seems to express something truly felt, whatever this may be. Furthermore, Hindu Professor Godbole is played in Lean's film by Alec Guinness, which perpetuates the questionable tradition of having Western actors play Indian roles – from Tyrone Power in the 1930s and 1940s adventure films to Keanu Reeves in Bertolucci's recent *Little Buddha*, where he plays prince Siddhartha, not forgetting Anglo-Indian actor Ben Kingsley, awarded an Oscar for his role as Gandhi.

Sara Suleri notes in reference to *A Passage to India* that this novel was partly inspired by the love Forster professed for Syed Ross Masood, Dr. Aziz's real-life counterpart. She argues, though, that its rhetoric is far more productively disturbing in the context of Forster's revision of an imperial erotic. In place of the orientalist paradigm in which the colonizing presence is as irredeemably male as the colonized territory is female, *A Passage to India* presents an alternative colonial model: the most urgent cross-cultural invitations occur between male and male, with racial difference serving as a substitute for gender (1992: 143).

In fact, even though women are the ones involved in the problematic relationships with Indian men, the rhetoric of imperial erotic focusing on the male body that Suleri alludes to, is clearly present in both *A Passage to India* and *Heat and Dust*, the films. There this rhetoric is easily identified because a great deal of the success of the films depends on the screen presence and the performance of the Indian actors in the main roles, Victor Banerjee as Dr. Aziz and Shashi Kapoor as the Nawab. Judy Davis, the actress who plays Adela Quested, appears to be – as one anonymous reviewer noted – alternatively pretty and plain, though the spectator is more likely to remember her bloody, torn clothes and her anguished expression after the Marabar incident rather than her serene beauty. In contrast, Banerjee is photographed so that his beauty is always emphasised, especially in the court room scene when his lawyer argues that molestation cannot be an issue since his defendant is obviously more attractive than Adela. Then she is at her worst, he at his best. However, compared to Edward Fox, who plays Fielding, Banerjee appears to be not effeminate, but certainly pretty where Fox is handsome, which means that the homoerotic imperial rhetoric Suleri detects in Forster's novel has been kept through the screen presence of the main male actors.

In *Heat and Dust*, Kapoor's Nawab is the very incarnation of the female fantasies expressed in popular romances. This is most evident in the scene – not included in the novel – in which Olivia first meets him. She happens upon him when he is getting dressed for the party he is to host; in his elegant, rich Indian clothes, Kapoor's body is fetishised and made to correspond to Western woman's sexual fantasies about dark, handsome, Oriental princes. Kapoor's sensuality centres on his expressive, manly face, so that, by contrast, blue-eyed, blond Christopher Cazenove – who plays Olivia's husband – seems handsome but bland, almost babyish. There is a shot of Olivia (played by Greta Scacchi) and her husband naked in bed, talking after sex, and what the camera shows are two very white bodies which look strangely similar (they are both face down); it is hard to imagine there is passion between those cold white English bodies. In fact, there is a certain parallelism between Olivia's husband and Adela's fiancée Ronnie, played by Nigel Havers: they are men who fail to satisfy their women and both films suggest that they can never compete against the allure Indian men pose for English women. Indeed, in the scene when the Nawab and Olivia finally make love, Kapoor and Greta Scacchi manage to convey sensuality and sexuality while keeping all their clothes on. In contrast, the almost casual way in which Anne's affair with her landlord is shot underlines the distance between the romantic, sensual past and the drab present – certainly, no descendant of Anne's would go back to India to trace her short-lived love story. Whereas Kapoor's face is memorable, Anne's lover is almost anonymous, merely the begetter of her child. Her child is thus an image of India Anne carries back to the West in a process by which the imperial erotic of Adela's hysterics and Olivia's sensuality becomes a post-colonial erotic of, I should say, selfish self-satisfaction. In this new rhetoric the Indian is not even a sexual object to be colonised but the excuse for the West to find sexual satisfaction in the creation of images of India – Anne's child – that are then cut off from their roots, from the deprived India represented by Anne's ignored lover. That is to say, colonisation is no longer presented as a sustained relationship, such as that between Fielding and Aziz or Olivia and the Nawab, but as a secretive affair in which India betrays itself, just like Anne's lover betrays his epileptic wife, and Britain, represented by Anne, may ignore her lover and keep a child she will bring up far from India.

The rhetoric of the imperial erotic is very different in *City of Joy*, though the choice of sex symbol Patrick Swayze as its protagonist is not casual. There is an emphasis, again, on the male Indian body, though the body of the main Indian character – Hasari Pal, played by Om Puri – receives attention not as a sexual object but in another exploitative context. Swayze's healthy American body is contrasted throughout the film with the sick body of Hasari Pal, a rickshaw puller, whose strength and health are sapped by his gruelling job. In Lapierre's novel, Pal's death is intended to convince Western readers that there is nothing romantic about poverty in India. In the film, however, Pal's tuberculosis is kept at bay; he is instead wounded by the third man in this pseudo-erotic triangle, a vicious gangster played by Art Malik. Swayze, as Doctor Max Lowe, has been trying to appropriate Pal's body by telling him how to treat his tuberculosis while ignoring to a certain extent the fact that it cannot be cured unless Pal gives up his job. The wound finally puts Pal's body in Lowe's hands, though it must be noted that Pal has previously saved Lowe from drowning in the monsoon flood.

There is some kind of indirect erotic bonding between the two men, as a gold chain Max is robbed of finally becomes part of the dowry of Pal's daughter. Amrita marries thanks to Max's gold, though this is kept secret by him; fittingly, the film ends with Max carrying Hasari away from his daughter's wedding to be cured of his bleeding wound, which seems to prefigure Amrita's defloration on her wedding night. The friendship Fielding and Dr. Aziz long for is achieved, but the roles are reversed: in *City of Joy*, the doctor is the foreigner, the patient is India in the person of Pal. Lowe cures more than wounds and he does it for free, out of pure gratitude, for Hasari and his fellow Calcutta citizens teach Lowe how valuable life is. Amrita's marriage is for him a satisfactory enough bond, which is why Lowe rejects Pal's offer of an arranged marriage to an Indian woman, seemingly choosing friendship over love.

Sara Suleri argues that too frequently "the rhetoric of otherness" is wrested "into a postmodern substitute for the very Orientalism that they seek to dismantle, thereby replicating on an interpretive level the cultural and critical fallacies that such revisionism is designed to critique" (op. cit. 12). This applies no doubt to Lapierre's novels and its film adaptation, though the novel is more honest, less sentimental than the film and, indeed, less biased than *A Passage to India* or *Heat and Dust*. How is, then, the growth of the fallacies that Suleri denounces to be avoided? Many readers of Said's *Orientalism* will have noticed that Said himself offers no alternative to the West's creation of the Orient. He notes that the gap between what the Orient is and the way it is depicted by the West is there "not so much because the language is inaccurate but because it is not even trying to be accurate" and adds that the Western writing that has defined the Orient "is a presence to the reader by virtue of its having excluded, displaced, made supererogatory any such *real thing* as "the Orient" (1991: 21). It is true that the films I have referred to perpetuate this state of affairs. Anthony Easthope argues that Said cannot say what the Orient is really like for "to do so would contradict its own argument". His book avoids, then, "placing the critic in the shamefaced position of speaking *for* the other" (1991: 134). But if the critic will not speak for the other and the channels of distribution of direct self-representations of India on film are so defective, how are stereotypes going to change? As things are, the West can only follow trial by error strategies in the representation of India, one of the many nationalities in the no longer politically correct invention of the Orient. Said himself gives us a clue, when he explains in *Culture and Imperialism* that the media are far ahead of the critics in altering the ways the nations of the world are perceived. "Our critical efforts", he writes, "are small and primitive, for the media are not only a fully integrated practical network, but a very efficient *mode of articulation* knitting the world together" (op. cit. 309). This is not, however, a solution, for the chances of nations other than the USA to dominate the media and other forms of expression such as film are right now nil. This is an explanation why there is a gap between the generalised denunciation of post-colonialism and the slow response of film and the media. It is unrealistic to imagine a scenario in which the media and film will suddenly become the perfect tools to transmit to other nations acceptable self-representations – if, indeed, there is such thing as an acceptable representation. As things are now, Hollywood dictates the reality of Spanish, Scottish and Indian films, just to take as examples three nationalities I have mentioned, because though British imperialism may be over, American imperialism is not. In this context, there arises a need to bypass the USA, but this is especially difficult to do in film and it must be noted that India is still relatively free of American influence in that area. In fact, India is one of the targets Hollywood is aiming at for further expansion abroad.

    As a conclusion, it can only be hoped that new channels of distribution will be found for Indian films, as they are an important means for India to publicise the image it wants to give the world. India is, however, not alone in this. All the nations face the same situation within American imperialism. What is also needed, and this is the most difficult point, is to bypass

American imperialism and to use the electronic postmodern world to circulate images of national identity that may stimulate the audience's wish to know other nations rather than to master them.

REFERENCES

Novels:

Forster, E.M, *A Passage to India* (1924), Harmondsworth: Penguin, 1985.
Jhabvala, Ruth Prawer, *Heat and Dust* (1971), London: Abacus, 1985.
Lapierre Dominique, *La Ciudad de la Alegría*, (*La Cité de la Joie*, 1985, trad. by Carlos Pujol), Barcelona: Seix Barral/Planeta, 1986.
Rushdie, Salman, *Midnight's Children*, London: Picador, 1981.

Films:

Gandhi (1982). USA/UK/INDIA
Director Richard Attenborough, Producers Richard Attenborough, Rani Dube
Screenplay Richard Attenborough
Cast: Ben Kingsley, Candice Bergen, Edward Fox, John Guielgud, Trevor Howard

Heat and Dust (1983). UK
Director James Ivory; Producer Ismail Merchant
Screenplay Ruth Prawer Jhabvala (based on her own novel)
Cast: Julie Christie, Christopher Cazenove, Greta Scacchi, Shashi Kapoor, Julian Glover

A Passage to India (1985). UK
Director David Lean, Producers John Brabourne, Richard Godwin
Screenplay David Lean (based on the novel by E.M. Forster)
Cast: Judy Davis, Victor Banerjee, Peggy Ashcroft, James Fox, Alec Guinness, Nigel Havers

City of Joy (1992). UK/FRANCE
Director Roland Joffe, Producer Jake Eberts

Screenplay Mark Medoff
Cast Patrick Swayze, Pauline Collins, Om Puri, Shabana Azmi, Art Malik

Other films mentioned:

Bernardo Bertolucci, *Little Buddha* (1994). UK/FRANCE
Secondary Sources:

Chakravarty, Sumita S, *National Identity in Indian Popular Cinema 1947-1987*, Austin: University of Texas Press, 1993.
Easthope, Anthony, *Literary into Cultural Studies*, London and New York: Routledge, 1991.
Said, Edward (1978), *Orientalism: Western Conceptions of the Orient*, Harmondsworth: Penguin, 1985.
Said, Edward, *Culture and Imperialism*, New York: Vintage Books, 1993.
Suleri, Sara, *The Rhetoric of English India*, Chicago and London: The University of Chicago Press, 1992.

INDEX